A User's Guide
to Democracy

A User's Guide to Democracy

HOW AMERICA WORKS

NICK CAPODICE and HANNAH McCARTHY

ILLUSTRATED by TOM TORO

CELADON
BOOKS
—
NEW YORK

A USER'S GUIDE TO DEMOCRACY. Copyright © 2020 by Nick Capodice and Hannah McCarthy. Illustrations copyright © 2020 by Tom Toro. All rights reserved. Printed in the United States of America. For information, address Celadon Books, a Division of Macmillan Publishers, 120 Broadway, New York, NY 10271.

www.celadonbooks.com

Author photographs, p. 355: Hannah McCarthy / *photo by Sylvia Wozny*; Nick Capodice / *photo by Justine Paradis*; Tom Toro / *photo by Cheshire Isaacs*

The Library of Congress Cataloging-in-Publication Data is available upon request.

ISBN 978-1-250-75184-3 (trade paperback)
ISBN 978-1-250-77994-6 (ebook)

Our books may be purchased in bulk for promotional, educational, or business use. Please contact your local bookseller or the Macmillan Corporate and Premium Sales Department at 1-800-221-7945, extension 5442, or by email at MacmillanSpecialMarkets@macmillan.com.

First Edition: 2020

10 9 8 7 6 5 4 3 2

From Hannah: For Joan and Larry McCarthy. You've always been the reasons why.

From Nick: For Marty and Redmond. And Marty.

From Tom: In memory of Jarvis Meach Babcock, who taught me about crops, crosswords, and citizenship.

CONTENTS

INTRODUCTION

Maybe you aren't 100 percent sure what the secretary of defense does all day. Or you're feeling a bit iffy as to what "free speech" actually means. Perhaps you've been pretending you know the definition of federalism.

What luck, then, that you've found yourself in possession of the basics of this democratic republic all in one place. This is your user's guide to American democracy, giving you the fundamentals on everything from the presidency to our election system to our basic civil rights. We parse the great hulking mass of our government into essential knowledge.

In order to enjoy and preserve this democracy, we have to know how it works. Understanding your rights as an American citizen can protect your job, your health, and your freedom. An awareness of the way things work around here is valuable armor. But it's a lot to remember, so we wrote it down in a book for you.

We do this for a living as the hosts of a public radio show and podcast, *Civics 101*. We guide people through the maze of

American democracy—from the Bill of Rights to executive privilege to Congressional investigations. Our show is a primer that leaves listeners better prepared to be engaged, aware citizens. *Civics 101* was started in 2016 as a response to a flood of questions coming into the station, including, "Can he/she/they really do that?" "What does the secretary of state do all day?" "What is the Defense Department?" and "How is the House different from the Senate?" It was a wonderful opportunity for us to admit we barely knew the answers ourselves, and to call up the experts who do. We've relied on the information we've gleaned from them to write this primer. The information in these pages was gathered from our country's most primary sources, the foundational documents, and what we found to be the most helpful of the nearly 250 years of scholarship and debate that have swirled around this democratic experiment since it first launched.

Within this book you'll find what we have learned over years of "wait, what?" and "so *that's* how it works," and "can you explain that to us *one more time*?" We've played democracy's interpreter so you don't have to. As far as your family is concerned, you've *always* understood the finer points of *McCulloch v. Maryland.*

SOME ASSEMBLY REQUIRED

THE POWERS
THAT BE

YOU CAN'T HAVE IT ALL

If there's one thing you have to know about the power structure of our federal government, it is that it, like Gaul, like Lear's kingdom, is divided into three. Our U.S. Constitution is the longest-surviving government document, and the first thing it does (after it says hello) is lay out who does what. This system is dependent upon the separation of powers and checks and balances. And these are not the same thing.

* Separation of Powers: This just means that our government is divided into three branches, and no branch has the same powers as any other; they are completely independent and complementary.

* Checks and Balances: This means that no branch of the government can be too powerful, as every major power can be checked, or blocked, by another branch. In James Madison's essay "Federalist 51," he said that in this system "ambition must be made to counteract ambition." He knew that politicians would be passionate about their ideals and would do anything to advance

them. These checks prevent one branch from unilaterally setting policy. Here's a diagram of how the branches keep one another in line.

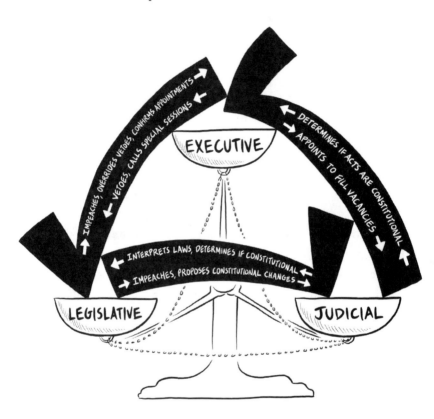

1

THE LEGISLATIVE BRANCH

At the outset, it seems like the House of Representatives and the Senate do pretty much the same thing.

Senators and representatives drive, walk, or take the secret tiny electric underground train to their respective chambers. There, they propose legislation, talk about it, and vote on it. But while they share many powers, these two houses are *not* both alike in dignity. Or perceived clout, at least. The length of terms, number of members, unique powers, and methods of legislation make the House and Senate as different as chalk and cheese. But before we do a side-by-side comparison, let's get some terminology out of the way.

WHAT WE TALK ABOUT WHEN WE TALK ABOUT CONGRESS

When we speak of **Congress**, we're talking about both the **House of Representatives** and the **Senate.** They are that mighty first branch, the legislative, whose powers are established in Article I of the Constitution.

> **CONSTITUTION 101:** Our constitution consists of seven articles written on four parchment pages. Article I, which establishes the legislative branch, gets far and away the most ink of them all, coming in at just over two pages by itself. And words are power! The more you have, the more things you can do. The founders clearly intended that Congress, not the president, was to be the most powerful arm of our government. That said, they also didn't want a complete legislative dictatorship, so they carefully explained what Congress could and could **not** do.

While they are both technically "houses," when we say "the House" we mean the House of Representatives. Those in the House are addressed as congresswoman/-man/-person. And while senators *do* work in Congress, they're addressed as "senator."

WHY TWO HOUSES?

Why not just have one house and be done with it? Why not a nice, pat, unicameral legislature that passes bills for the president to sign? Well, that was how we did things under the Articles of Confederation,[1] our much maligned first constitution. And to be fair, there are some successful one-house legislatures out

---

[1] The Articles of Confederation was our first governing document, and it was in effect from 1781 until 1789, when our constitution was ratified. It had a one-house Congress, no executive branch, and very few federal powers, and was referred to as a "firm

there (lookin' at you, Nebraska!), but the bicameral system was born as a solution to one of the fiercest debates at the Constitutional Convention . . .

THE GREAT COMPROMISE

When the fifty-five delegates from twelve colonies (Rhode Island was a no-show[2]) were hammering out our new system of government in 1787, there arose a seemingly insurmountable issue of representation. How many people from each state should be elected to Congress? Before the convention even started, James Madison had drafted the Virginia Plan (also

---

league of friendship" between the states. They didn't even have a common currency! You'd have to trade your Connecticut shillings for Rhode Island dollars at the border!

[2] It's not because they weren't invited. Rhode Island was famous for its streak of independence and resistance to a stronger federal government. They even earned the nickname "Rogue Island" for being the one state that didn't show up.

called the "Randolph Plan" or the amusingly blunt "Big State Plan"), which said that representation in Congress should be based on "the number of free inhabitants." Enslaved Americans would initially not be counted toward apportionment. A big whanging state like New York would therefore have many times the power of a state like Delaware. The smaller states were more likely to back William Paterson's New Jersey Plan (only referred to as the "Little State Plan" when New Jersey wasn't in the room), which gave each state one vote, regardless of its size. And thus we got to the Great Compromise, where one house, the House of Representatives, was proportionate to the population of free inhabitants in each state, with enslaved people counting as three-fifths of a person (Native Americans not counting at all), and the other chamber, the Senate, consisting of two people from each state.

CONSTITUTION 101: The three-fifths compromise, within Article I, Section 2, Clause 3, is one of the two places slavery is mentioned in the Constitution, the other being its abolition within the Thirteenth Amendment. One of the most contentious battles about representation in the House was whether to count enslaved people (who had no vote) as part of the population. If they were counted, that would dramatically increase that state's presence in the legislature. James Wilson, a vocal opponent to slavery, proposed that enslaved people should count as three-fifths of a person for purposes of representation. This compromise secured southern support for the Constitution, but gave slave-states inordinate legislative power.

So that's how we got here.

REPRESENTATION AND TERM LIMITS: THE HOUSE

There are 435 members of the House of Representatives. Each one represents a chunk of a state, called a Congressional District.

> **GERRYMANDERING:** Gerrymandering (a word that comes from combining former Vice President Elbridge Gerry with "salamander") is drawing Congressional Districts to favor one party or the other. A nice little case history of this is the 2016 Congressional Election, when there was about a fifty-fifty split of popular votes for Republican and Democratic reps. But due to those maps, the Republican party gained forty more seats in the House.

That number, 435, was chosen as a cap by the Permanent Apportionment Act of 1929. The number of reps from any state, however, can change.

For example, California has fifty-three reps now, but it only had thirty in the 1950s.[3] If one state loses a Rep due to a decreasing population, some growing state will snap it up.

As to term limits, they are two years. No representative is safe. Every two years, all 435 of them are up for reelection.

---

[3] After the census every ten years, we parcel out our 435 reps. We give one rep to each state and then dole the rest of the 385 out one by one using a nifty and atrociously complicated formula based on state population.

BUT WHAT DOES THAT MEAN?

That means the House can be a wild and crazy place. A place that is subject to the ever-changing whims of the American people.

Because the House is refreshed so frequently, its representatives can campaign and vote on hot-button, often controversial issues. From the Anti-Masonic Movement[4] to the Tea Party to the Green New Deal, the House has a rich history of people elected to shake things up.

Likewise, because they each represent their smaller Congressional District and not the entire state, house reps are more familiar with their constituents.

The price that the House pays for its closeness to the people is its reputation as the "lower house," because they each represent fewer people and hold less power. But they are every bit as important to our government as the lofty Senate.

SENATORS ARE ALLOWED TWO FROM EACH STATE.

---

[4] This was a real thing, a party entirely devoted to abolishing the Freemasons. None of them got a Senate seat, but forty were elected to the House of Representatives.

REPRESENTATION AND TERM LIMITS: THE SENATE

No complicated mathematical formula needed! Two people from every state. One hundred total.

Term limits are a little trickier in the Senate. A senator is elected for a whopping six-year term, but these terms are staggered, so every two years about a third of them are up for election. Senators belong to Class I, II, or III. This isn't a ranking of any kind, it just determines when they're up for reelection. Class II is up for election in 2020, Class III in 2022, and so on. Two senators from the same state are *never* in the same class. This was designed to ensure there's some living memory in the Senate, so that when the new kids come to town there's a majority that's been there for some time already.

> **CONSTITUTION 101**: But it hasn't always been this way! The original text of the Constitution said, "The Senate of the United States shall be composed of two senators from each State, chosen by the Legislature thereof." They were elected by the state legislators, not by the people! In the early 1900s there was a growing fear that senators were buying their seats from corrupt state legislatures. The Seventeenth Amendment, ratified in 1913, changed those words "chosen by the Legislature thereof" to "elected by the people thereof."

BUT WHAT DOES THAT MEAN?

Senators have a nice long stretch in office, and therefore don't have to start campaigning ten minutes after their acceptance speech. Because they represent an entire state, there is less room for radicalism, and leaders in the Senate work hard to quell any members who try to buck the party line.

The staggered election of senators has an *enormous* impact on our government. The Classes were divvied up during our first Senate in 1789, and when new states were added to the union, their two Senate seats were assigned the next available Classes, by drawing lots if it was more than one state at a time.

And the ramifications of this? Let's say the Senate is pretty evenly split between the parties; if the Class that's up for election is mostly from very conservative states, you're going to get a Republican Senate majority with relatively little effort.

And finally, because Democrats have more voters in big cities, the Senate tends to swing more conservative. New York City has millions of Democrats, but their state gets just two senators, same as the dozen less-populated, more-Republican-dominated states.

WHO GETS TO DO IT: THE HOUSE

It's pretty lax, actually! The Constitution says any American who is twenty-five or over, lives in the state they're trying to represent, and has been a U.S. citizen for at least seven years can run for office.

WHO GETS TO DO IT ACTUALLY

In 1786, the average age of a member of the House was forty-five years old. That number has risen steadily ever since, with the 115th Congress, from 2017 to 2019, being the oldest in history, averaging 57.8.

But while the trend is old, white, wealthy, and male, the 2018 election ushered in a significantly younger House. Incoming members of Congress in 2018 were on average forty-seven years old, a full decade younger. The 116th Congress is also the most diverse in U.S. history, although there is clearly still a long way to go: 106 women, fifty-five Black Americans, forty-five Latinx Americans, twenty Asian Americans, and four Native Americans.

Money is certainly important in a House campaign, but not as important as it is for the Senate. In competitive House races in 2018, the mean spending on campaigns was about 4 million dollars. Since you're representing a portion of your state, name recognition in your district is the most important thing. This is gained through local television ads and radio spots, plastering roads with campaign signs, attending events, and, most of all, knocking on doors.

Finally, it helps to be a Christian. According to a poll from the Pew Research Center, 53 percent of the current House is Protestant, 32 percent Catholic, and 1.4 percent Mormon. There are only three Muslims and one Buddhist. Fourteen members of the House answered "Don't Know" or "Refuse to Answer" on the poll.

WHO GETS TO DO IT: THE SENATE

The rules are a little more stringent for the Senate, but not overwhelmingly so. The Constitution states in Article I, Section 3, that a senator must be thirty years old, nine years a U.S. citizen, and an inhabitant of the state they are running in.

WHO GETS TO DO IT ACTUALLY

While the aforementioned traits of being white, wealthy, old, and male help you out in the House, they really help out if you're running for the Senate. And this is in no small amount related to the staggering amount of money you need to raise to run a Senate campaign. The average is over $10 million. In the narrow 2018 race for a Senate seat from Texas, Ted Cruz spent $45 million and Beto O'Rourke spent $78 million.

So, *very* wealthy. And if you want to know how white, take a guess at how many Black people have served in the entire history of the Senate.

Yup, ten. That's all. As of this writing, there have only been ten Black people in the U.S. Senate.

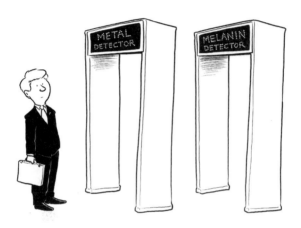

Race and religious faith break down along similar lines as they do in the House, just with a significantly smaller portion of non-white and non-Christian senators. Two interesting stats, however, are gender (a full 25 percent of the Senate is female) and occupation (50 percent—half!—of our senators previously served in the House of Representatives). Just like it helps to have been a senator to be a president, working in the House is a way to get your foot in the senatorial door.

SHARED POWERS

- Both Houses have one power above all else: **Make the darn laws that run our country.**

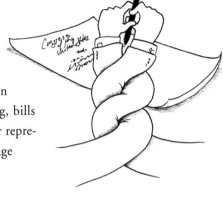

The process for that differs in each, but basically speaking, bills are proposed by senators or representatives: a small percentage get voted on in one chamber; and if they are passed, they cross over to the other chamber. If they pass there, too, they go to the president, who then signs them into law or vetoes them. A veto kills a bill, unless two-thirds of both the House and Senate vote to override it, in which case it becomes a law without the president's signature.

- ★ Either House can initiate constitutional amendments.

- ★ With a two-thirds majority in both Houses, they can together override a presidential veto.

- ★ Every year the president submits a budget request to both Houses, and they each write and vote on their own budget resolutions.

- ★ Either House can pass a resolution to declare war,[5]

---

[5] Presidents can't declare war. They are, however, the commander in chief of the armed forces, and (according to the War Powers Resolution) as long as they inform Congress within forty-eight hours and Congress authorizes it, they can send armed forces wherever they deem fit.

which they've done eleven times. The last time was against Romania in 1942.

* Likewise, either House can establish and levy taxes for the support of an army.

* Congress establishes rules about immigration and naturalization.

* And finally, they can coin money (as in mint quarters, dimes, nickels, and pennies), print dollar bills, and regulate interstate commerce.

One important point about the powers of Congress: If the rules aren't specifically outlined in the Constitution, they can be altered. Every two years, the new Congress writes its rules. They can create new committees, new protocols for bringing bills to the floor, and even new rules for the filibuster. Thus, the information on the following pages is by no way set in stone. One of the most interesting things about our government is that while the Constitution is ironclad and very difficult to amend, the way the three branches wield their power is malleable and has changed over the centuries.

UNIQUE POWERS: THE HOUSE

• Initiate money bills.

If you're like most of us and enjoy the gentle clink of a fat leather satchel of coins hitting the bar at the tavern, you'll enjoy the expression "the power of the purse." While both Houses initiate bills, only the House of Representatives can initiate bills regarding federal spending.

CONSTITUTION 101: Article I, Section 7 says, "All Bills for raising Revenue shall originate in the House of Representatives." But there are ways around this. The Senate can take a proposed bill from the House, gut everything, and change it to be about raising money wherever they want. Sure, it was technically initiated in the House, but it has zero actual House content. *Also*, all bets are off if the president declares a National Emergency. Money can come from just about anywhere when that happens.

These bills can give money, like an appropriation bill to a government agency, or they can eliminate funding.[6]

• Break a tie.

Three times in history, none recently,[7] there was a tie for electoral votes for president. The House is charged with breaking that tie. It takes 270 votes to win, and it seems improbable to have a 269/269 tie in an election, but a "tie" includes when no party gets to that magic number. In 1968, the pro-segregation Independent George Wallace got forty-eight electoral votes, which wasn't enough to force a tie, but proved it could happen again with a strong third-party candidate.

---

[6] For instance, in 1974, the House passed the Foreign Assistance Act, which *ceased* all funding for aid and military support in South Vietnam, directly leading to the capture of Saigon and the end of the war.

[7] Most recently, the House chose the president in the absolute circus that was the Hayes/Tilden election of 1876. Republican Rutherford B. Hayes had 165 electoral votes and Democrat Samuel J. Tilden had 184, but there were twenty votes in dispute. House Republicans and Democrats struck a deal; Hayes was given those twenty votes, and the Republicans in return removed federal troops from the South. This compromise ended the Reconstruction era, allowing white Democrats to regain power in the South and disenfranchise Black voters.

- Initiate impeachment.

The tools of investigation! Any member of the House can initiate impeachment with a resolution and start the ball rolling. It goes to the House Rules Committee and then the House Committee on the Judiciary, who investigate grounds of impeachment and report back to the House for a vote. And unlike in the Senate, where it takes a two-thirds majority to convict, the House requires just a basic majority of votes to impeach.

If the house votes "yea," then the individual has been impeached, which just means "accused." It then goes to the Senate, where the trial takes place, and only *then*, if the Senate votes against them, will the individual be removed from office, and possibly prevented from holding federal office again. This is why even though impeachment proceedings have happened about sixty times, only twenty of those have made it through the

House, and only a meager eight have made it through the Senate, resulting in the official being removed from office. And while we may think of it as being something reserved for presidents, all eight were federal judges.

Three presidents have been impeached in U.S. history: Andrew Johnson (for violating the Tenure of Office Act, replacing his secretary of war before his tenure was up), Bill Clinton (for lying under oath and obstruction of justice regarding a sexual relationship he had with Monica Lewinsky), and Donald Trump (for abuse of power and obstruction of justice regarding his soliciting of election assistance from Ukraine). Richard Nixon was going to face impeachment for obstruction of justice regarding the Watergate break-in, but resigned upon learning he lacked the votes in the Senate to prevent removal.

UNIQUE POWERS: THE SENATE

- Confirm appointments.

This power is not found in the weighty first Article of the Constitution, but in Article II, Section 2. And it's often called the "advice and consent" power. The text reads that the president "shall nominate, and by and with the Advice and Consent of the Senate, shall appoint Ambassadors, other public Ministers and Consuls, Judges of the Supreme Court, and all other Officers of the United States." So the president picks, and the Senate gives the thumbs-up.

And while Supreme Court Justice nominees and Cabinet nominees get the most attention, there are about two thousand political offices that require appointment.

The nomination goes to its relevant committee, which can opt to hold hearings and vote to move it right to the floor for debate or vote to not move it to the floor.

The Senate majority leader then decides if and when this nomination will be voted on by the entire Senate.[8] After debate (more on that later), the question is asked, "Will the Senate advise and consent to this nomination?" And 99 percent of the time, that nominee is confirmed.[9]

- Treaties.

Like confirmations, the Constitution says the president makes treaties with the advice and consent of the Senate. Unlike confirmations, it requires a whole two-thirds of the Senate to concur. They don't ratify the treaty, they approve or reject the president's

---

[8] As of this writing, Senate confirmations are not subject to the filibuster and require a simple majority, fifty-one votes, to succeed. There is one exception. Supreme Court nominees are subject to the filibuster, which we'll get to in a moment, but the long and the short of it is that it requires sixty votes to succeed.

[9] One snag in the confirmation process can be **Senatorial Courtesy**, which is not about using the proper fork or putting your jacket on a puddle; rather, it's when, if a senator is against a nomination and is both from the same state as the nominee *and* of the same party as the president—a single nay vote from that senator kills the nomination. The thought behind this is that the senator probably knows that nominee pretty well, and since they're in the same party as the president, they have nothing to gain by stopping this nomination. This isn't written in the Constitution, or even the Senate Rules, but it goes all the way back to George Washington, when he nominated Benjamin Fishbourn of Georgia to the post of naval officer. Georgia Senator James Gunn, who was no big fan of Fishbourn, stood up and said he wouldn't vote for him.

resolution, or approve it pending required changes. And also like confirmations, treaties are usually approved. There have been only twenty-one rejections out of the 1,500 or so treaties sent to the Senate.

One reason for this is that only noncontroversial treaties get sent to the Senate in the first place. This is because the United States has a unique caveat to treaties, which is that they don't necessarily have to happen. A treaty is an agreement with one or more nations that enters international law. And while the formal process requires the Senate's approval, presidents can issue "executive agreements" which do not. And "executive agreements" happen about ten times as often as treaties. More on these in our section on the executive branch.

- Try impeachment cases.

Impeachment doesn't mean removal from office, it just means the official is formally charged. What the House started, the

Senate must finish. With the exception of presidential impeachment, the Senate runs the trial by themselves. Members of the House of Representatives act as prosecutors, presenting evidence to the Senate, who also act as jury. If two-thirds of the Senate give a guilty verdict, the official is removed from office.

In the rare occurrence of a president being put on trial, the chief justice of the Supreme Court steps in and runs the proceedings. But they're not in any way similar to a judge in a courtroom proceeding. They cannot rule on their own, they do not determine rules of evidence, and everything is at the whim of the Senate majority.

- Elect the vice president in case of a tie.

Just a quick historical side note: Until 1800, the vice president didn't run with the president. The person who became vice president was the presidential candidate who got the second-most electoral votes. But the Twelfth Amendment changed all that, stating that the president and vice president were to be elected separately, and if there was a tie for VP, the Senate got to choose. And it happened exactly one time.

EXECUTIVE BRANCH 101: In 1836, our well-sideburned eighth president, Martin Van Buren, won the presidential election. But his running mate, Richard Mentor Johnson, did not get enough VP votes to secure the job; he needed 148 and got 147. The Twelfth Amendment stated that if one candidate did not get enough votes, the Senate must pick from the top two candidates. Which they did. Johnson became the ninth VP and went on to break fourteen ties in the Senate.

We doubt we will ever see this again, since the standard now is that they both run on a shared ticket. But again, a "tie" can come from when no candidate gets the majority of Electoral College votes, meaning a strong third party can bring this power back into play.

HOW THINGS ACTUALLY GO: THE HOUSE

Let's start with one fact: Of all the bills and resolutions proposed in the House, about 3 to 5 percent become law. And that low percentage has been pretty standard ever since we got on this merry-go-round in 1789.

Of that small number, the vast majority are what are considered "noncontroversial bills." Naming a post office. Creating a holiday. Authorizing states to issue an electronic duck stamp.

> **LEGISLATIVE BRANCH 101:** HR 1206, the Permanent Electronic Duck Stamp Act of 2013. Sadly, it was not about regulations regarding waterfowl-themed postage, but issuing permits for duck hunting.

It's not that the House is afraid to pass radical, swooping bills. It's just that it's not in their best interest to go forward with something if it's clear that it won't pass in the House, let alone the Senate. A bill only needs a simple majority vote to pass on the House floor, but it rarely gets there.

Once a bill is proposed, it goes to a committee or a subcommittee, where it is, most of the time, postponed, abandoned, or forgotten. The lucky few that survive are researched in committee, debated, marked up, amended, and are sent to a Rules

Committee (another committee!) to determine how they will be considered on the House floor. There are 435 people ready to weigh in, so debate time is strictly limited, and both debate and proposed amendments to the bill must be *germane*—they must be relevant to the piece of legislation. You can't go sneakin' a Christmas goose into a bill on highway maintenance. But most of the time, there are no amendments at all, and so-called "debate time" is limited to as little as fifteen minutes. Once the rules are set, it's ready to put on the House calendar for a vote.

And you'd think, after all of this, after that poor bill has suffered the death of a thousand cuts, it would be ready finally to be trotted out for a vote. But there's one last snag. A bill can be on the calendar, but the Speaker of the House decides which ones come to the floor on any given day. The schedule is always tight, and that bill can be pushed to the back of an overfull dance card, where it is kept waiting in the wings in its finest suit, only to be thrown out when the two-year session ends.

LEGISLATIVE BRANCH 101: There is a way to get a bill to the floor in spite of the speaker of the House (or, more often, the head of a committee who is stalling the process), and it's called a discharge petition. These are extremely rare, but they've happened a handful of times. If a bill has been introduced and assigned to a committee for at least thirty days, half (218) of the House can sign a literal petition. These signatures are public information. And once 218 signatures have been collected, that bill is taken out of committee and put on the floor for a vote.

Bills have an expiration date. Every two years, Congress starts anew with a clean slate. So regardless of how far along a bill was in the process, it'll have to start again from the very beginning.

Let's look at the House of the 115th Congress, from 2017 through 2018.

* 9,871 bills were proposed.
* 1,371 got a vote.
* 1,322 passed in the House.
* 322 also passed in the Senate.
* 302 were signed by the president into law, 3.4 percent.

When representatives propose bills, they show their constituents that they are *doing things*. They are people of *action* and *beliefs*. And while that may be true, the process can grind even the most earnest ideals to dust.

But that's not necessarily a bad thing. At the end of this chapter we'll tell you why.

HOW THINGS ACTUALLY GO: THE SENATE

If you walk away with one tidbit of how things differ in the House and the Senate, let it be this. The Senate was created for debate. That is, unless we're talking about a noncontroversial bill, where a senator can move for "unanimous consent," and if every single voting member agrees, the bill can be passed with no debate, amendments, bill-reading, anything. This happens an awful lot.

But if a more controversial bill makes it to the Senate floor, unlike in the House, where discussion on bills is strictly timed and must be relevant, there are *no restrictions whatsoever* on topic or time. There isn't even a Rules Committee! When bills get to the floor for a vote, Senators can talk about them for as long as they wish. Or any other matter. And here we enter the most important, much maligned, ever-changing land of . . .

THE FILIBUSTER[10]

Hoooo, doctor, here we go. Turn on the steam bath and put in your arch supports.

---

[10] You can't skip a little pirate etymology! The word "filibuster" comes from the Dutch *vrijbueter,* which meant "buccaneer in the West Indies." This also got anglicized into the word "freebooter." The Spanish adapted it into *filibustero* and the French *filibustier.* It is assumed that the definition regarding obstructing government ment was first used in the 1850s, as these lawmakers "pirated" legislation and took over the ship of government.

LEGISLATIVE BRANCH 101: In 1957, Senator Strom Thurmond broke the record for filibustering when he spoke for twenty-four hours and eighteen minutes to block a Civil Rights Act. Prior to his walk to the dais, he took steam baths to remove as much fluid from his body as possible so he wouldn't have to urinate. There was a bucket strategically placed in the cloakroom in case of an emergency.

Until 1917, any member of the Senate could hold the floor as long as he wanted to delay voting on a bill. This became a tool for the minority to stall legislation of the majority. But the Senate changed their rules in 1917, creating something called *cloture,* whereby debate could be ended immediately if two-thirds of the Senate agreed. They did this because other Senate business could not happen while a bill was being debated, so a filibuster would bring the chamber to a complete standstill. This rule, created to protect the minority from being steamrollered, took on new power in the late 1950s and early '60s, when Southern Democrats who opposed Civil Rights legislation brought the Senate to a standstill with myriad filibusters. The passage of the Civil Rights Act in 1964 came after the Senate overcame a filibuster that had stalled any other legislation in the Senate for over *sixty days.*

In the wake of these Civil Rights filibusters, the 1970 Senate put a "two-track" system in place, whereby another piece of legislation could be on the floor on the same day, with time split between the two. This weakened the power of the filibuster to halt the gears of the Senate, but it made filibustering much easier to do, since you only had to do it for half of the day. Likewise, the number of votes needed for cloture was lowered from two-thirds to three-fifths, meaning you only needed sixty votes to stop a filibuster.

One of the most recent changes to the filibuster is something referred to as the "nuclear option," where the Senate can vote to change its rules in certain circumstances to circumvent this sixty-vote requirement. In 2013, the Democrat-majority Senate voted that the filibuster would no longer be allowed for executive appointments *except* for nominations to the Supreme Court. And in 2017, the Republican-majority Senate extended that provision to the Supreme Court. Both parties altered the Senate rules to help their side; the Democrats to prevent filibustering of every appointee by President Obama, and the GOP to speed through President Trump's Supreme Court nomination of Neil Gorsuch.

BUT WHAT DOES THIS MEAN?

It technically only takes a majority, fifty-one votes, to pass a bill in the Senate. But unless we're dealing with a presidential appointment, it is taken as a given that someone will filibuster. It is simpler to do, and has become the norm for any bill that has political significance. We've reached a point where senators no longer need to stand up and read recipes for fried oysters and crawfish (which Huey P. Long did in 1935) to stop a bill from being voted on. All that needs to happen is that a member of the opposing party inform the Senate majority leader that there are forty-one senators opposed to this bill, and the mere *threat* of a filibuster is enough to prevent the vote.

So while the number to win in the Senate is fifty-one votes, nobody will consider pushing a bill to the floor unless they think they have sixty.

And, perhaps the most important thing of all, *none of this matters* if the Senate majority leader doesn't want something to be voted on. Discharge petitions are even less successful than in the House. If the Senate majority leader doesn't want something to be voted on, the bill is almost certainly dead.

TELL ME THE GOOD NEWS

If the preceding pages angered you at all, if you dislike that it seems more likely to win a $3 trifecta at the Kentucky Derby than to get a bill through both chambers, maybe we can provide some cold comfort.

The inefficiencies in the House and the Senate seem like a bug, **but they're actually the whole point**. This system is set up to prevent any radical movement or ideology from taking over and changing everything overnight. It takes people voting on issues in election after election to get anything done, waiting up to six years to replace a senator that they disagree with.

If efficiency is what you're after, the most streamlined style of government is despotism: a system where a single entity makes every decision, and nobody disagrees with anything and everything gets done with the snap of a finger. Our system may seem complicated and messy and slow, but that's exactly how the framers wanted it.

And remember, when we're talking about things like the filibuster, or getting a vote onto the floor of the House, or a majority leader keeping a motion from even being debated—these are things that can change with any Congress, and it's up to us to hold our representatives accountable to alter the rules we don't like. Ultimately, because they know we select them, it is in their best interest to listen to us. But they don't feel this pressure unless we make our opinions heard.

So give them a call. Their number one job is to listen to you.

2

THE EXECUTIVE BRANCH

THE LEADER OF THE FREE WORLD[1]

In September of 1962, forty thousand onlookers sweated in the Texas sun as the famously un-sweaty president[2] squinted and

---

[1] The term "free world" first showed up in the papers during World War II. The Allied Powers saw themselves in stark contrast to the fascism of the Axis—compared to Germany, Italy, and Japan, the Allies said, we live in a free world. Heck, we *are* the free world. By the Cold War, the new enemy of freedom was Communism. Of the fancy free democracies out there, the U.S. was the richest and loudest. So we got the prize!

[2] On September 26, 1960, Vice President Richard Nixon squared off against the dashing young Massachusetts senator, John F. Kennedy, in the nation's first-ever televised presidential debate. Nixon was getting over the flu, running a fever, pale from a hospitalization for an injured knee, and exhausted from campaigning. Kennedy had a perma-tan and had been holed up in a hotel room resting and preparing for days before the debates. One guy looked sweaty and sick, the other glowy and well-rested. Also handsome. Very handsome. Former Senator Bob Dole later recalled thinking Nixon sounded great on the radio, but looked rough on the screen. It's unclear if the American public held it against Nixon, but Kennedy did end up winning the election by a slim margin and Nixon refused to do televised debates in his following runs, in '68 and '72.

grinned. John F. Kennedy was there at Rice Stadium in Houston to make a promise: that the United States of America would go to the moon within the decade. To the *moon*. A mortal man promised an entire country that they would land a ship on a rock in space. The best we'd done at that point was orbit our own planet. It was an audacious promise. And yet, seven years later, that promise was fulfilled.

Question is, did Kennedy give us the moon? Or was it Nixon, who was President by 1969 when we took that one small step for man? Does the president have the power to take us to the moon? Or anywhere, for that matter?

Yes and no.

WHO GETS TO DO IT?

Were you to come across a want ad for our nation's leader, it might look a little something like this:

College degree? No need. Prior experience? Nope. Convicted felon? Go right ahead. On paper, it's easier to become the U.S. president than it is to score most entry-level jobs.

WHO *REALLY* GETS TO DO IT?

Sure, Zachary Taylor had never touched politics before running for president. Abraham Lincoln was famously unschooled.

Barack Obama didn't get much done as a senator. But when it comes down to it, most of the time it takes a pretty fancy pedigree to make it into the White House.

Money, power, know-how, and know-*who* are practically prerequisites for the job with almost no prerequisites. Ivy League educations, successful military careers, and political office have decorated, in one way or another, every individual to hold the office of the presidency. And while not all presidents were wealthy before they ran, it takes money to raise money. If you want a star-spangled campaign, you'd better be hobnobbing with some fancy-pants folks. The kind whose credit cards weigh more than the average hardcover book. Oh, and it has tended to help if you're white and a man.

CONSTITUTION 101: A word on "he." You'll notice that's how we refer to the president. That is for simplicity's sake in following the language of the Constitution, which refers to the president as a he, and only as a he. Article II, however, uses the

gender-neutral "person" when specifying who can apply for the job, and nearly all Constitutional law scholars agree that a woman can be president. For a long time, the shes and theys of the world have been throwing their hat into the ring for a seat at the Resolute desk, and judges are staying mum. In actual fact, women were running for president in the United States before women were permitted to vote in the presidential election in all states. Victoria Woodhull is considered to be the first, though she was just thirty-four years old when she ran, likely making her 1872 candidacy invalid.

WHAT THE PRESIDENT DOES

The president's job description can be found in Article II of the U.S. Constitution: the executive branch. In our government, we've split the power up across three branches to avoid something pesky like an authoritarian government drunk on its own power wine. Coming off the wild monarch ride that was Great Britain, the Constitutional framers agreed that an executive was needed but were wary of making him too king-like. In the end, their scheming gave us one person with a lot of hats behind a big desk in an office with no corners. Those hats—not all official—include:

* Chief executive.

* Commander in chief.

* Chief of state.

* Chief of party.

* Chief diplomat.

* Guardian of the economy.

* Legislative chaperone.

Some of these hats are ten gallons large, while others are closer to a beret.

CHIEF EXECUTIVE

The main power vested in the U.S. executive branch is to take care that federal laws are enforced, and the president is the head of that branch. We've interpreted this to mean that the president has both the duty and the power to enforce federal laws.

> CONSTITUTION 101: This power can be found in Article II, Section 3—it's come to be known as the "Take Care Clause," tucked in at the end of a long list of seemingly unrelated powers and responsibilities. All we get is "he shall take care that the laws be faithfully executed." As with most of our Constitution, the guys who wrote it went with the as-vague-as-possible technique and left us to squabble over it for centuries to come.

Duty: He is supposed to respect the laws that Congress passes and make sure they're followed,[3] by himself and his agencies.

---

[3] Presiding over the massive executive branch, the president is supposed to make sure that, say, federal tax laws passed by Congress are enforced by the IRS. But Congress is also responsible for providing the president with the resources to accomplish that enforcement. So unless the IRS is provided with way more money, they're limited to prioritizing the big baddies of tax evasion even as lower-level federal offenses are happening.

Power: He and his agencies have some discretion not to enforce a law if they believe it is unconstitutional.

Sound mutually exclusive? Welcome to Constitutional law, friend.

APPOINTMENTS

Being chief executive means that the president is technically in charge of the four million employees of the executive branch. Naturally, a little delegation is in order to make that work, and so the president chooses individuals to manage the agencies and bodies that comprise the branch. The president gets first-draft pick for every appointment he makes.

Take the Cabinet, for instance. The vice president, fifteen executive department heads, and a team of special advisors all get a seat at the table if the president says so (more on these top dogs later). Our chief executive also appoints:

* Ambassadors.
* Agency heads.
* Committee heads.
* U.S. attorneys.
* Supreme Court judges.

Sound a little like Hammer-of-Thor, Trident-of-Neptune, Thunderbolt-of-Zeus-level delegation power? The president gets to nominate whomever he wants to high positions, but all of the above have to be approved by the Senate unless they pass a law saying otherwise.

COMMANDER-IN-CHIEF

The commander-in-chief clause is one of the more "you figure it out" moments of the U.S. Constitution. We're told that the president is commander in chief of the Army and Navy and state militias if they're called into service. We've since looped the Air Force into that as well.[4]

Is the president a member of the military? Nope. He's a civilian. The fanciest civilian in the country.

Can the president declare war? Most definitely not. That's for Congress to decide.

Does the president make the rules for the military? Also no. Also Congress.

What sorts of things *can* he do as commander in chief?

* Command troops and order operations in times of war.

* Launch a nuclear strike.

* Appoint, promote, and fire military officers.

* Deploy troops inside the country to put down domestic unrest.

* Repel attacks against the U.S.

* Order retaliatory invasions and attacks.

* Implement changes in military policy.

EXECUTIVE BRANCH 101: Inside a forty-five-pound briefcase carried by a military aide are the means—codes, menu of

---

[4] The Air Force isn't in the Constitution because human flight didn't come around until the twentieth century. So when we finally did bring the military to the skies, there was some discussion as to whether or not the Air Force was *unconstitutional*.

options—that would allow a sitting president to launch a nuclear attack. It's called the "football," and it is never far from
the president's reach. To verify his identity, the president has
a special code on a plastic card that he keeps in his wallet.
The card is called the "biscuit," and President Bill Clinton once
lost his for several months. We feel ya, Bill. We lose our keys
several times a day! Except our keys can't scorch the earth.

If this is beginning to sound like the president can, in fact,
wage war without Congressional approval, that's due to a little
thing called "police action"[5]—basically, committing troops and
engaging in warlike behavior without call-
ing it war. Congress has not declared war
since World War II. Yet the United
States has engaged in wars in Korea,
Vietnam, Iraq, and Afghanistan in the
decades since, often with the sitting president committing troops and ordering
strikes without Congressional approval.

All of this is a matter of Constitutional interpretation, historical
precedence, and legislation that has

---

[5] Although the Supreme Court has not ruled on police action, Congress did pass
the War Powers Resolution in 1973 (Richard Nixon tried to veto it, and Congress
overruled his veto). After U.S. involvement in the Korean and Vietnam Wars,
legislators wanted to reel in the president's ability to initiate or escalate military
action abroad. The Act requires that presidents notify Congress after deploying
troops and limits how long engagement can go on without Congressional approval. Every president since has considered the Act unconstitutional and basically
said, "Nah. I'm gonna do what I want."

broadened the president's power to use military force. Call it "police action" instead of "waging war," and you can Houdini your way out of that Constitutional straightjacket.

LEGISLATIVE CHAPERONE

If you're going to put one person in charge, the founders figured, it might not be the best idea if that same person made all the laws. Et voilà, a perpetual wrestling match between POTUS[6] and Congress, between the person who promised you all sorts of gleaming possibilities when you voted for him and the people who can make those possibilities a reality.

The Constitution is clear on this one: Congress makes the laws. So why do presidents make such a *thing* out of their legislative goals?

For one thing, POTUS is one of the most visible and influential people on the planet. So when the president—as required by the Constitution—gives Congress information about the state of the union,[7] he also tells them his legislative agenda and then spends the rest of the term lobbying Congress to get it done. A lot of the time, at least part of that agenda comes to fruition.

---

[6] OTUS (of the United States) started as a telegraph abbreviation back in the day when you paid by the word, and was typically just used to talk about POTUS (the President of the United States). Later on, it's rumored that the secret service used "FLOTUS" (First Lady) as code to refer to Nancy Reagan. "SCOTUS" (Supreme Court) and, occasionally, "VPOTUS" (Vice President) followed suit. Though "VP" ultimately won out as the abbreviation for vice president, pronounced as "veep."

[7] George Washington and John Adams did deliver the state of the union in the form of a formal address to Congress, but Thomas Jefferson opted to just send a letter rather than hoof it to Capitol Hill. This became tradition until Woodrow Wilson opted for an in-person address in 1913.

And then there's that bona fide Constitutional power: the veto.[8] Every bill that passes the House and the Senate ends up on the president's desk, and he can sign it, ignore it (making it a de facto law), or reject it and send it back to Congress with his objections.

Now, if that was all there was to it, it would make the president the most powerful entity in lawmaking. It might also make for some tyrants, which we're not super into as a country. So Congress can override a veto and pass a law with a two-thirds majority in both Houses.

CONSTITUTION 101: The president has ten days (excluding Sundays) to review and sign or not sign a bill. If he vetoes the bill and Congress has adjourned in that ten-day period, a wacky little something called the pocket veto occurs and Congress can't do anything about it save go over the whole process all over again to get a bill through. These days, Congress makes a point of preventing the pocket veto by not officially adjourning. Congress overrides fewer and fewer vetoes lately, mostly because the president won't issue it at all if he knows it'll be overridden. Unless, of course, he's trying to make a point.

Speaking of power . . . the president does have this thing called an executive order, in which he tells an executive agency what to do. That's how all of America's steel mills were seized and

---

[8] For a while at the beginning of the nation, the veto was only used when the president considered a bill unconstitutional or noticed some spelling mistakes. This all changed when Andrew Jackson openly admitted he was using his veto power on bills that he didn't agree with politically.

nationalized in 1952[9], and how the segregated military was integrated in 1948. Congress can undo these power moves, but it's convoluted and pretty rare. They can either pass a law that invalidates it or refuse to pony up the funds to carry it out. If they do pass a law, of course, the president can just veto it. It'd then take a supermajority to override the president's veto, and at that point you might be making yourself look bad by picking a fight with the leader of the free world.

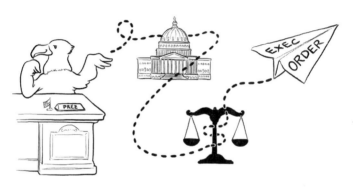

CHIEF OF STATE

The office of the presidency carries a "he shook my hand and I'm never washing it again" kind of star power. As chief of state—an unofficial role—the president serves as the poster child for the United States. Our number one spokesperson, our most honored

---

[9] Harry S. Truman ordered the seizure of the nation's steel mills when steel workers threatened a strike over federally imposed wage and price controls during the Korean War. Truman insisted this was necessary to maintain the production of crucial weapons and ammunition. Steel mill owners sued and the Supreme Court ruled, in *Youngstown Sheet & Tube Co. et al. v. Sawyer,* that Truman's order was unconstitutional.

luminary, our most famous celebrity. The president does not just defend the Constitution, he represents it. He is supposed to stand for American democracy.

In some countries— Great Britain, for example— the head of state (king or queen) serves as a symbol  while someone else runs the government. Around here, the same guy who pardons a Thanksgiving turkey can pardon a convicted federal felon. The ceremonial jobs, while vital to keeping up the president's image, are less official (and way more fun) than most of what the president does. These ceremonial responsibilities generally include:

* Throwing the first pitch of the baseball season.
* Welcoming foreign dignitaries to the U.S.
* Waving to children at the White House Egg Roll.
* Awarding the Presidential Medal of Freedom.
* Hosting a party for college football champions.
* Planning their own funeral in the first week in office.
* Buying a dog to seem more relatable.
* Getting roasted at the Correspondents' Dinner.
* Giving speeches.

CHIEF OF PARTY

Political parties don't show up anywhere in the Constitution, but let's get real. That donkey and that elephant make the free world go 'round. As party chief (there are fewer balloons and cakes involved than you would think), the president wields his star power to get his people elected and make his party as appealing as possible.

In order to win America's top political gig, the president has to first convince constituencies around the country that he's amazing and his ideas are, too. He has to make powerful special-interest groups believe that he will make their dreams a reality. Once in office, the president can wield those supporters to his advantage in order to strengthen his party. He endorses and campaigns for candidates—sometimes even convinces people to run. The more people from the president's party who sit in Congress, the more likely it is that the president will be able to pass his agenda.

As chief of the party, the president is allowed to appoint the chair of his party's national committee. He can also fire that chair at will, and replace them with someone else. This means that the president's national committee tends to give him what he wants. Suddenly it's not just the Democratic party or the Republican party—it's Mr. Kennedy's Democratic party, Mr. Eisenhower's Republican party.

There is a catch to all of the above, though. An unpopular president might find himself without an invitation to the pool party. Hanging with an uncool president can mess with your social status (i.e., your chances of getting elected). It's junior high all over again. If a president's approval ratings start to tank, he could become something of a pariah in Washington, where legislators don't want voters associating them with an unpopular party leader. Jimmy Carter, for example, was a political outsider lacking a strong base, was considered weak on foreign policy, and presided over an economy that was plagued by inflation and unemployment. All of this meant that even though his own party controlled both House and Senate, Carter had trouble getting his policies through Congress.

CHIEF DIPLOMAT

If you've ever watched *The West Wing*, you know that most of the backroom wheelings and dealings, the negotiations with foreign powers, the cool secret meetings at Camp David are because of *this*. Being the number one diplomat in the nation is basically like being chief of state but instead of hanging with baseball players and throwing the first pitch of the season, you're hanging with the most powerful people on the planet and making deals.

As chief diplomat, the president is constantly hosting other diplomats, jet-setting all over the world to shake fancy people's hands, and trying to set foreign policy. If he manages to make an agreement official, it might fall under the treaties clause[10]—and like a lot of what the president gets to do, he needs two-thirds of the Senate to approve. Treaties are formal, written agreements between nations, and they can be about just about anything, including:

* Peace.
* Trade.
* Independence.
* Reparations.
* Territory.
* Human rights.
* Immigration.
* The environment.

Presidents, and the U.S. in general, are really big on striking deals. Treaties galore! It's the ratifying and abiding by the treaties that we tend to have a little trouble with. Starting with the hundreds of (largely unequal) treaties with Native Americans that we broke or changed, we've had a tendency to push for big, shiny handshakes and then do the cool guy fake out at the last minute. Still, we ended the American Revolution with a treaty. We bought

---

[10] Article II, Section 2, in the Constitution.

Alaska from Russia with a treaty. Woodrow Wilson even declared us the *savior of the world* with the treaty that ended World War I . . . we just didn't feel up to ratifying that treaty ourselves. It takes the Senate to ratify a treaty, and senators at the time were afraid that signing the treaty and thereby joining the League of Nations would drag the U.S. into international conflict in the future.[11]

There are a handful of treaties you should familiarize yourself with, as they changed the nation (and sometimes the whole world) big-time.

The Treaty of Paris of 1783

Ended the Revolutionary War after being negotiated by Ben Franklin, John Adams, and John Jay. A friend of Franklin tried to make a painting of the signing, but the British declined to sit for it. The result was an unfinished painting, a visual representation of the irreparable divide between the former colonies and Great Britain.

Treaty of Greenville of 1795

Ended the Battle of Fallen Timbers and made twelve Native American tribes give up their land—most of present-day Ohio and Indiana. This began the practice of annual payments made to tribes who gave up their lands. Many Native American individuals, including the iconic Tecumseh, criticized this move and fought to maintain territory in the Northwest.

---

[11] Only forty-eight countries in total joined the League of Nations, by the way, which ultimately failed in its primary goal of preventing another world war. The League disbanded in 1946, and its mission was transferred to the far more successful United Nations, which had been established the year before.

Louisiana Purchase

There was a time when France controlled basically the entire middle of the modern-day U.S. Not super great for a country that is starting to think, hey, we want to just keep walking west and taking stuff until we fall into the Pacific. Also, President Thomas Jefferson really wanted access to the Mississippi River and Gulf of Mexico for trading. So he sent James Monroe to Paris to ask for New Orleans, and Napoleon was like, what about the whole dang thing? Fifteen million dollars later, we had acquired about 800,000 square miles of U.S. territory.

Treaty of Ghent

The British may have signed a treaty to end the Revolutionary War, but that didn't mean they were totally simpatico with the baby United States. The UK kept getting in the way of trade and territory expansion, so it was war, again, this time in 1812. Britain burned the capital, Francis Scott Key wrote "The Star-Spangled Banner," and then Russia stepped in to say, "Hey, you crazy kids. You can work this out." The Treaty of Ghent, signed on Christmas Eve in 1814, called the War of 1812 quits.

Treaty of Guadalupe Hidalgo

You know how France owned the big, beautiful middle of the country until we bought it? Well, Mexico owned another one-sixth or so. The Mexican-American War was a battle for borderlines that ended with the fall of Mexico City, Mexico's surrender to the United States, and the signing of the Treaty of Guadalupe Hidalgo. With it, we purchased (for another $15 mil) California, Nevada, and Utah, and parts of Arizona, Colorado, and Wyoming.

Mexico also agreed to give up its claim to Texas and recognize the Rio Grande as the southern border of the United States.

The Treaty of Paris of 1898

Could be the food, the architecture, the romance—however you slice it, we just love making treaties in Paris. And this one ended the Spanish-American War, resolved a key issue in that war (Cuban independence—they got it!), and resulted in the U.S. acquiring Puerto Rico, Guam, and the Philippines.

The North Atlantic Treaty of 1949

This treaty resulted in an organization of the same name: the North Atlantic Treaty Organization, a.k.a. NATO. Twelve nations (later joined by another seventeen) got together to agree to protect one another, initially, from the Soviet Union. It came with a mutual self-defense clause that wasn't actually enacted until the September 11th attacks on the U.S.

And then there are these things called "executive agreements," where the president makes an international deal without asking the Senate what they think. How is that different from a treaty, you ask? Well, it isn't, really. As long as he doesn't break any existing laws, the president can make all sorts of international pinky promises. These executive agreements can be done in secret, too, with the president only mentioning it to Congress after the fact.

> **CONSTITUTION 101:** The Constitution doesn't say anything about executive agreements. But in the 1937 case *United States v. Belmont,* the Supreme Court ruled that POTUS does indeed have the power to execute executive agreements without Senate consent and that these agreements carry the same weight as treaties even

if they aren't treaties in name. Still, most executive agreements do get Congressional approval through a joint resolution. The "sole executive agreement" is a rare but totally legal bird born of the president's foreign relations responsibilities. That said, an executive agreement does have force of law and is supposed to extend only to things a president could do without Congressional consent anyway.

GUARDIAN OF THE ECONOMY

This one isn't an official role, but we dare you to try to be president without talking about job growth and the economy.

The economy ends up being a blame game with the president. If he's lucky and things are looking good, he might even get re-elected because of it. But if things are looking not so good, well that's another story

But does the president really have that much sway over the economy? It is the president who appoints the chair of the Federal Reserve, and the Fed is supposed to ensure economic stability and long-term growth. It's the president who proposes a budget to Congress, and that budget can have lasting impacts on inflation, exchange rates, and taxes. It's the president who wrestles with Congress for years on end trying to get financial policy on the books. So while the president can't directly mess with our money, he can certainly nudge things in the right (or wrong) direction.

Fair or not, the guy is gonna get blamed when we can't afford even one measly slice of avocado toast. Or, you know, a house.

THE OTHER PERKS OF THE JOB

* Convene Congress in the case of an emergency—and adjourn them as deemed necessary.

* Grant pardons and reprieves for people convicted of federal crimes (can't pardon *himself* in the case of impeachment, though we're still not sure if he can pardon himself of criminal acts outside of impeachment).

* Declare a state of emergency or federal disaster area.

* Create or dismantle federal agencies through executive action.

* Exercise executive privilege and refuse to disclose information—this includes refusing to disclose certain information to Congress if he feels that it would be against the best interests of the country.

* Be tried for "treason, bribery, and other high crimes and misdemeanors" and, if convicted, be removed from office and possibly banned from holding any future federal office—this is a possible conclusion of impeachment. Removed from office, mind you, but not incarcerated.

* Recognize foreign governments.

* Promise we'll go to the moon.

PRESIDENTIAL PRECEDENT

When you consider what the president does versus what the Constitution says the president can do,

there's a wide sea of discrepancy. Constitutionally speaking, the president can do only a handful of things by himself: serve as commander in chief, grant pardons, appoint some officials, and veto bills. Almost everything else requires Congressional input or approval. So where does all of that executive power actually come from? A generous understanding of presidential discretion.

As presidents have asserted powers not explicitly prohibited in the Constitution, they have broadened—and strengthened—the reach of the executive office. Some have influenced the Constitution itself. Others triggered Supreme Court cases. Some of these powers remain unofficial—never codified, yet adhered to nevertheless. All because the most powerful person in the world did it.

All presidents have the potential to set precedents and change the office, but there are some who have done so with tremendous effect. Others have set precedents that have yet to be imitated by their successors—still, once a president has opened the door, it's that much easier for another to walk through it.

GEORGE WASHINGTON—UNTRODDEN GROUND (FIRST)

* Appointed a Cabinet.

* (Executive) ordered executive department heads to submit reports.

* Proposed legislation to Congress.

* Preferred "Mr. President" to "His Excellency."

* Retired after serving eight years.

WE CAN LOOK PAST THAT WHOLE "OWNING SLAVES" THING, RIGHT?

ANDREW JACKSON—AN INDEPENDENT EXECUTIVE (SEVENTH)

* Vetoed more than anyone had before him—including the first pocket veto—and did so simply because he disagreed with them, not just because he considered them unconstitutional.

* Forced out Cabinet members—both those who desired to succeed him and those whose spouses would not socialize with a friend's new and scandalous wife.

* Handicapped the central bank without Congressional approval.

* Rewarded loyal followers with appointments.

* Nudged the executive branch toward equal footing with Congress.

ABRAHAM LINCOLN—"WAR POWERS" (SIXTEENTH)

* Claimed that the president had broad powers in moments of crisis.

* Suspended habeas corpus (the right to an appearance in court) without Congressional authorization, allowing for the arrest of political opponents without a court hearing.

* Blockaded southern ports without Congressional consent (an act of war).

* Expanded the army (a Congressional duty).

* Freed millions of enslaved people via executive order.

I LITERALLY DIED IN A THEATER, BUT HAMILTON GETS THE BROADWAY TREATMENT?!

THEODORE ROOSEVELT—THE FIRST MODERN PRESIDENT (TWENTY-SIXTH)

* Threatened to use federal troops and settled a nationwide coal strike.

* Lobbied for sweeping changes to federal government.

* Made the presidency a celebrity position.

* Brokered peace between Russia and Japan.

* Created national parks and monuments by executive order.

I ALSO INVENTED MERCHANDISING! (TEDDY BEAR ®)

WOODROW WILSON—THE SCHOOLMASTER IN POLITICS (TWENTY-EIGHTH)

* Had a doctorate in political science.

* Worked closely with Congress to craft and pass bills.

* Held first presidential press conference.

* Established the Federal Reserve and Federal Trade Commission.

I GIVE MY PRESIDENCY A PASSING GRADE.

* Asked Congress to declare war on Germany.

* Helped negotiate the Treaty of Versailles.

* Escalated discriminatory hiring policies and segregation of Washington, D.C., offices.

FRANKLIN D. ROOSEVELT—THE BOSS (THIRTY-SECOND)

* Served four consecutive terms (the Twenty-Second Amendment term limits followed six years after his death).

* Closed the banks by executive order.

* Ordered Congress to convene and deal with the banking crisis of the Great Depression.

* Drafted and sent legislation to Congress—his New Deal programs empowered the government to regulate the economy.

* Dramatically expanded White House staff to aid in drafting legislation and foreign policy.

* Bonded with the public through radio broadcast "fireside chats."

LYNDON B. JOHNSON—BIG DADDY (THIRTY-SIXTH)

⭐ Designed the "Great Society" through legislation that promoted civil rights, Medicaid, Medicare, public services, and funding for the arts and education.

⭐ Launched the "War on Poverty" through forty pieces of legislation designed to improve the living conditions and economic opportunities afforded to low-income Americans.

⭐ Pushed for the Voting Rights Act to prevent the disenfranchisement of Black Americans in the South.

⭐ Shocked the nation by dropping out of the 1968 presidential election—aside from Calvin Coolidge, the only president not to seek a full second term.

GIDDYUP.

BARACK H. OBAMA—THE AUDACIOUS ONE (FORTY-FOURTH)

⭐ First African-American president.

⭐ Publicly endorsed same-sex marriage.

⭐ Appointed a former first lady (Hillary Clinton) to his Cabinet.

⭐ Appointed a Latina woman to the Supreme Court.

⭐ First sitting president to have a Twitter account.

I PRESCRIBE HOPE AND CHANGE.

DONALD J. TRUMP—THE REALITY T.V. PRESIDENT (FORTY-FIFTH)

* First president to assume office without any prior military or political experience.

* Crossed the demilitarized zone and met with the leader of North Korea while in office.

* Used Twitter to issue tens of thousands of official White House statements.

* First president to turn seventy before assuming office.

A HEARTBEAT AWAY: THE VICE PRESIDENT

John Adams, the first vice president of the United States, once observed of his prestigious role, "My country has in its wisdom contrived for me the most insignificant office that ever the invention of man contrived or his imagination conceived." Harry Truman summed it up a bit less delicately, calling the role about as useful as a "cow's fifth teat."

The vice president has exactly one Constitutional job. He is president of the Senate. Mostly without voting power. The job is literally an afterthought that came after Constitutional framer Roger Sherman noticed that the vice president would be "without employment."

VEEP

The Constitution fails to tell us what the president of the Senate is expected to do, however, so that was left up to the Senate to decide. They took a boring job . . . and kept it really boring.

The VP is supposed to sit at a desk and preside over—a.k.a. sit and watch—Senate proceedings. He can't formally address the Senate without permission. He *does* get to vote to break a tie in the Senate (some vice presidents get dozens of chances to do this), but it isn't especially common. Most of the time, the VP doesn't even show up and a stand-in called the *pro tempore* Senate president does the job.

The reward for this practical oblivion? Well, you get a house on the grounds of the U.S. Naval Observatory. You get a tidy salary. And sometimes, about 20 percent of the time in history up to this point, you get to become the president of the United States of America.

If the president dies, or quits, or is removed from office, the vice president takes over. This has happened eight times in history. And then there was the time that Nixon resigned in Deep Throat disgrace and Gerald Ford took on the mantle. But for the most part, the VP will wait in the wings and never step onto the stage.[12]

To be fair, things used to be a lot worse. Before the Twelfth Amendment, the vice president was simply the guy who came in second in a presidential election. As a member of the legislative branch (president of the Senate), the vice president was for a long while considered forbidden from participating in executive branch work. Theodore Roosevelt mused about the benefits of giving the VP a place in the Cabinet . . . and then seemed to kind of forget about it when he became president himself.

CONSTITUTION 101: A new plan for electing the president and vice president, the Twelfth Amendment replaced Article II, Section 1, of the Constitution and switched up the Electoral College. The amendment was proposed when Thomas Jefferson (a Democratic-Republican) got second billing to John Adams (a Federalist), and finally passed in 1804 after Jefferson had tied with Aaron Burr in the bizarre election of 1800.

It wasn't until Teddy's distant relative Franklin Delano demanded that he—and not the party's National Convention, as

---

[12] Before John Tyler assumed the presidency in 1841 upon the death of William Henry Harrison, it wasn't clear exactly what it was going to mean when a VP stepped in for an indisposed president. Would the VP be merely an acting president? Would they get full presidential powers? We got our answer, as we so often do, through precedent. John Tyler insisted on full presidential powers and he got them, setting the stage for the few who would follow in his footsteps.

had been the custom—choose his running mate that the office started to change. Harry Truman was consulted by FDR now and then. Lyndon B. Johnson got a space in the executive office building. And finally, Walter Mondale scored an office in the White House and suggested to Jimmy Carter that perhaps the vice presidency did not *have* to be the most pathetic, depressing job in government.

Carter said okay.

Ever since, vice presidents have covered everything from advising the president and conducting foreign diplomacy to crafting policy, attending funerals on the presidents' behalf, and negotiating with Congress.

It all comes with one little caveat. The VP is only a cool kid because the president says so. If you want a seat at the table, you better stay on the boss's good side.

SERVING AT THE PLEASURE OF THE PRESIDENT

This oft-repeated phrase means, basically, that the president giveth, and so too he can taketh away. Like that secretary of state gig? It can vanish in an instant if POTUS gives the nod. Don't get too comfortable, Madame District Attorney. That cushy desk job is hanging by a thread.

The president has the power to dismiss, at will, pretty much anybody he also has the power to appoint (with the exception of federal justices, who are members of the judicial branch and can only be removed through impeachment, and independent agency heads, like the chair of the Federal Reserve).

But the officers of the executive branch? Open season, year round.

Who comprises this vast forest of termination targets, you ask?

THE EXECUTIVE OFFICE OF THE PRESIDENT OF THE UNITED STATES

Headed by the White House chief of staff, the EOP can be reorganized by the president whenever he pleases. This means that the agencies that comprise it now could change. The role of the agencies and organizations within the office is to support the work that the president is trying to get done, starting with the **White House Office,** which consists of all of the people in the West Wing who work directly for the president. The **National Security Council** advises the president on matters of, well, national security, while he gets his economic policy intel from the **Council of Economic Advisors.** The **Council on Environmental Quality** helps to coordinate environmental efforts at the federal level here on Earth while the **National Space Council** advises on national and international space policy. The **President's Intelligence Advisory Board** advises the president about the state of intelligence collecting in the U.S. and tells him whether international intelligence gathering is, ahem, legal. The **Office of Management and Budget** is the biggest agency in the EOP, and it's in charge of creating the president's budget and making sure programs and policies are complying with it. The **Office of National Drug Control Policy,** headed by the most impressive executive title, the drug czar, coordinates national and international anti-drug efforts on the part of the executive branch. Science and technology advising happens through the **Office of Science and Technology Policy** while the **Office of the U.S. Trade Representative** both advises the president on trade and conducts trade negotiations. And the entire executive office is managed by the **Office of Administration.** The **Office of the Vice President** falls under the EOP umbrella and that's about all it does.

THE CABINET

Fifteen principal offices and a handful of other department heads around one long oval table. It isn't the entirety of the U.S. government, but a lot of what we're provided—and what regulates us—comes from the executive branch.

Department of State
Run by: The Secretary of State

This is the agency in charge of foreign affairs, from how we conduct ourselves to how other nations conduct themselves. This is the delicate operation of existing, as peaceably as possible, in a world that does not always like our loud voices and NASCAR and giant breakfasts.

No pressure or anything. Just diplomacy at the highest possible level, led by . . .

- **The Secretary of State,** who serves as POTUS's principal advisor on foreign policy and the appointing and dismissing of ambassadors, ministers, and consuls.

They oversee operations such as:

- ⋆ Conducting foreign affairs negotiations.
- ⋆ Issuing passports to U.S. citizens.
- ⋆ Recognizing foreign consuls so they can operate in the U.S.
- ⋆ Going to international conferences.
- ⋆ Negotiating treaties.
- ⋆ Protecting U.S. citizens abroad (if you, say, found yourself in a pickle in Mumbai).
- ⋆ Supervising U.S. immigration law abroad.

* Promoting international economic relations.

* Supervising the Foreign Service (comprised of the thousands of people who help the DoS do all of this stuff abroad).

* Telling Congress and American citizens about what is going on in other countries.

* Possessing and managing the Great Seal[13] and preparing certain presidential proclamations and treaties.

Department of the Treasury
Run by: The Secretary of the Treasury

The Treasury is in charge of U.S. financial security. No big thing.

It's got nine bureaus that carry out 98 percent of the work it does. The other 2 percent lands in the lap of . . .

* **The Secretary of the Treasury,** who advises the president on fiscal matters—the rest is taken care of by:

* **The Alcohol and Tobacco Tax and Trade Bureau,** which collects excise[14] taxes on firearms and

---

[13] It took fourteen guys six years to come up with the Great Seal of the United States (we use it for treaties and other important documents). It's that spreadeagle under a sun made of stars clutching a bundle of thirteen arrows in the left talon and an olive branch in the right, protected by a flag-ish shield, with a ribbon in its beak that reads, "E Pluribus Unum" ("Out of Many, One"), and only the State Department can use it.

[14] An excise tax is an indirect tax that we place on all sorts of things that we consider unnecessary (excise taxes are often referred to as "sin" taxes here in the U.S. Your favorite wine might reasonably be valued at $10, but you're paying $12 because the vineyard is charged a $2 excise tax on the manufacture of it.

ammunition, and enforces and administers laws covering the production, use, and distribution of alcohol and tobacco.

- **The Bureau of the Fiscal Service** provides accounting, collection, and financing services—basically, they deal with public debt.

- **The Bureau of Engraving and Printing** designs and manufactures currency and securities (a catchall term for stocks, bonds, mutual funds, and other investments). These are the guys who print out sheets of cold, hard cash. But they don't do the coins—that would be the job of . . .

- **The U.S. Mint.** The cents to the BEP's dollar. They make the coins you find under the driver's seat next to that old french fry and the sunglasses you thought were gone for good. They also make bullion—gold, silver, platinum, and palladium coins that you can buy and bury in your backyard if you're interested in playing the precious metals market.

- **The Financial Crimes Enforcement Network**—their motto? Follow the money. These are the guys who are going to notice if you've been bad with money. Not like you missed a student loan payment. More like you've been money laundering. Or evading your taxes. Or financing a terrorist organization. They investigate your financial crimes and sic law enforcement on you.

- **The Inspector General**—we have a lot of Inspectors General in these here States United. Each agency has one, and at the Treasury, the IG conducts audits and investigations to make sure everything's aboveboard in the agency.

- **The Treasury Inspector General for Tax Administration**—oh look, another one! The TIGTA oversees the Internal Revenue Service and watches for fraud or abuses of power.

- **The Internal Revenue Service.** Old friend. This is the biggest bureau in the Treasury, and they collect federal income taxes from you and us during the annual spring cleaning of our wallets.

- **The Office of the Comptroller of the Currency** makes sure that banks around the country are following the law. They issue rules and regulations, and they get to decide whether your bank application is approved.

Department of Defense
Run by: The Secretary of Defense

Where does the president keep his armies? In his sleevies. And by "sleevies" we mean the Pentagon, the largest office building on the planet. This is the headquarters of the DoD, the department tasked with deterring and winning wars, and providing security for the U.S. and our allies with our Army, Navy, Air Force, and sometimes Coast Guard.

At the tippy top of this behemoth (well, a rung below the *tippy* POTUS top) is the . . .

- **Secretary of Defense.** Because those framers wanted to ensure the military was civilian-run, this role cannot go to anyone who's been in the military within seven years of appointment. This role is the primary policy maker for the DoD and sometimes thought of as a deputy commander in chief, ranking higher than combatant commanders of the U.S. military. The SoD works side by side with . . .

- **The Inspector General of the Department of Defense,** who investigates the DoD, makes sure programs are running as they should, and lets the Secretary and Congress know if something is amiss. The DoD IG advises the secretary on policy that will keep things running smoothly, along with:

- **The Department of the Army** and **the Secretary of the Army**

- **The Department of the Navy** and **the Secretary of the Navy**

- **The Department of the Air Force** and **the Secretary of the Air Force**

- **The Joint Chiefs of Staff,** ranking military officers who advise the president and secretary of defense but do not have command powers, and:

- **The Combatant Commanders of the Combatant Commands,** who are the ones taking orders from the president and secretary, and passing them on to either a geographical region of command (U.S. Africa Command, U.S. Indo-Pacific Command) or a function (U.S. Cyber Command, U.S. Transportation Command).

All of the above is guided by the Great and Powerful Title 10 of U.S. Code[15]—this is what provides the legal basis for all roles and missions of the armed forces of the United States.

Department of Justice
Run by: The Attorney General

The blindfolded lady of the executive department, this is the long law-enforcing arm of the United States. The DoJ has the

---

[15] The U.S. code comprises the general laws of the United States. Though the Constitution is the Supreme Law of the Land, it's pretty short. The U.S. code is where you find all of the other federal laws that govern this fair nation, and Title 10 is a big one. Title 10 provides the legal basis for the organization, roles, and mission of the Army, Navy, Air Force, and special reserve forces of the U.S. military. It also establishes the military justice system, which operates separately from the civilian system.

power to handle all criminal prosecutions and civil suits in which the U.S. has an interest.

This department is complex—forty-two different components—the most important being . . .

- **The Attorney General**—*not* the president's lawyer—the country's lawyer. Also the chief law enforcement officer, so technically a top cop. The AG does advise the president and Cabinet on legal matters and is in charge of all the **Attorneys General, U.S. Attorneys,** and **U.S. Marshals** throughout the United States. Sometimes the AG represents U.S. interests in the Supreme Court but usually that's done by the **Solicitor General.** The AG is also the boss of:

- **The Federal Bureau of Investigation,** designed to protect us from terrorist attacks, foreign espionage, cyber attacks, public corruption, international crime, threats to our civil rights.

- **The Drug Enforcement Administration,** keeping smack off the streets. Or trying to, anyway. The DEA investigates people and organizations who violate controlled-substance laws, traffic in illicit substances, commit violence as manufacturers or distributors of illicit substances, etc.

- **The Bureau of Alcohol, Tobacco, Firearms, and Explosives,** taking care that the public is protected from illegal firearms, alcohol, and tobacco trafficking and trying to protect us from the violent use of bombs, guns, and gangs. "Explosives" was added in 2002—we still tend to refer to this one as the "ATF."

- **The Bureau of Prisons**—if you get convicted for breaking federal law, this is the office that's overseeing your incarceration. They're supposed to make sure all federal prisons are safe, humane, secure, and cost-efficient, and provide reentry programs for federal offenders once released.

Homeland Security
Run by: The Secretary of Homeland Security

The newest kid on the block, this department was a direct response to September 11th and established only eleven days after the attacks. Congress made it official in 2002 with the Homeland Security Act.

Whereas the Department of Defense is mostly committed to military action abroad, the Department of Homeland Security is around to secure home base with the aid of . . .

- **The Transportation Security Administration** (TSA), a national security agency that keeps the lines long and the skies (and roads and tracks) safe—the idea is to maintain freedom of movement while protecting travel in the U.S. In the year 2000, you could bring a four-inch blade onto an airplane. No kidding.

- **Immigration and Customs Enforcement** (ICE) is supposed to enforce federal criminal and civil laws concerning border control, customs, trade, and immigration, including removing certain undocumented individuals from the country, and investigating the illegal movement of people and goods and transnational criminal groups. ICE does not patrol borders, however. That's the job of their sister agency:

- **Customs and Border Protection**—there to prevent terrorism and maintain legitimate trade and travel. They're also supposed to stop drugs, traffickers, and contraband from coming over the border. CBP is made up of what used to be a bunch of disparate agencies.

- **Citizenship and Immigration Services,** which administers naturalization and immigration services.

- **Federal Emergency Management Agency,** an older agency (around before the HSA), designed to respond to emergencies that overwhelm state and local governments.

- **Coast Guard,** the oldest continuously operating seafaring agency in the government, which conducts search-and-rescue operations at sea, enforces maritime law, protects ports, and monitors the environment.

- **Secret Service**—originally established to combat counterfeiting in the U.S., the Secret Service still investigates financial and web-based crimes. It wasn't until after the assassination of William McKinley in 1901 that Congress asked the Secret Service to protect the president. They now protect the president, his immediate family, former presidents, their spouses and any children they have under the age of sixteen, major presidential and vice presidential candidates, and visiting heads of state.

Department of the Interior
Run by: The Secretary of the Interior

The most introspective of the executive departments, but think more sensitive outdoorsy parent-type than moody teenager. The Department of the Interior, run by the **Secretary of the Interior,** speaks for the trees, if you will. And the lumberjacks who want to cut them down.

It is our primary conservation agency, dedicated to protecting and managing our natural resources and cultural heritage. It includes:

- **The Bureau of Indian Affairs,** the oldest agency in the department and oh boy has it been a learning curve. Beginning with Residential Schools and unprotected treaties, the organization today is supposed to promote a better quality of life and economic opportunity for "American Indians, Indian tribes, and Alaska Natives," while protecting assets—millions of acres of land and sub-acres of minerals held in trust for American Indians.

- **The Bureau of Land Management,** which manages the "land nobody wanted"—in other words, the land that Manifest Destiny-ers passed up on their way to greener western pastures. They're in charge of protecting and utilizing the giant chunks of public land scattered across the states.

- **The National Park Service,** which protects and preserves national parks, monuments, battlefields, seashores—everything from Edgar Allan Poe's house to the White House. And all while wearing those rad ranger hats and avoiding the typical American indoorsy pallor.

- **U.S. Fish and Wildlife Service,** which enforces federal wildlife laws, preserves existing habitats, and tries to improve habitats for the birds and the bees and the bears and the elusive and adorable Gulf Coast Jaguarundi.

- The DoI also protects and manages the responsible use of dams in the West, "submerged lands," a.k.a. *the ocean that we happen to own,* and coal mines, and tries to figure out what to do about this whole climate change thing.

Department of Agriculture
Run by: The Secretary of Agriculture

Otherwise known as the people who figure out how to keep us, and the people who want our food, fed.

The USDA came around to keep American farming alive and well, and eventually began to ensure that the consumption of that food also kept us alive and well, through:

- Disaster relief and broadband access for farmers, ranchers, and people in rural areas; soil and water conservation; agriculture research; and wildfire prevention.

- Farming economic policy.

- Managing school nutrition standards.

- Ensuring that American-produced meat, poultry, and eggs are safe to eat.

- Managing food-assistance programs for women, infants, and children (WIC) and the Supplemental Nutrition Assistance Program (SNAP), which also help farmers get rid of excess crops and keep prices high.

- Scientific and technological advances on the part of USDA scientists (think seedless grapes, orange juice concentrate, and trying to remove allergens from peanuts).

Department of Health and Human Services
Run by: The Secretary of Health and Human Services

These are the folks who are trying their best to keep us healthy. The goal is to protect our health and provide services to those of us who need assistance most, their first line of defense being the . . .

- **U.S. Public Health Service,** which includes the **U.S. Public Health Service Commissioned Corps,** which is tasked with preserving the health of the American public. The **Assistant Secretary of Health,** if a serving member of the PHSCC, becomes the highest-ranking member of the corps and a four-star admiral when they're appointed to the job. The **Office of the Surgeon General,** who is in charge of disseminating health information to the American public, is within the office of the assistant secretary of health.

- **Food and Drug Administration**—wait, isn't the USDA in charge of food? Kinda! The FDA looks out for everything the USDA doesn't—so everything except meat, poultry, and eggs. Even that is a little murky—the FDA, for example, deals with whole eggs in shells, while the USDA deals with the stuff on the inside, like packaged egg whites. Chicken feed? FDA. Chicken farm? USDA. Don't worry about it, they're trying their best. The FDA also ensures the safety and efficacy of human and pet drugs, medical devices, cosmetics, and products that emit radiation. In 2010, Congress also gave the FDA the power to regulate tobacco in order to try to stop tobacco companies from marketing cigarettes to minors.

- **National Institutes of Health,** doling out grants to organizations and fancy minds who can come up with genius stuff like 3D-printed brains. They give money to the smarties who make our lives longer and our illnesses more tolerable.

- **Centers for Disease Control and Prevention.** The CDC are the ones keeping an eye out for disease outbreaks, whether they're the result of human error or purposeful attack, and doing the research into communicability, treatment, and vaccines that they can pass on to us in an attempt to protect us from everything from mushroom-borne listeria to, say, a worldwide pandemic.

HHS also handles:

- Medicaid and Medicare.

- Some federal assistance for families and children.

- Substance abuse and mental health services.

- The registry of toxic substances and diseases.

- Indian health services.

- Federal health policies.

Department of Commerce
Run by: The Secretary of Commerce

Feeling a little redundant here? Don't we already have the money people in the Treasury? Yes—we've got folks to pay our nation's bills (and make sure we pay ours . . .) but the Department of Commerce is here to keep capitalism happy.

- **The Secretary of Commerce** represents U.S. businesses within the Cabinet and tries to promote a healthy business economy. This is the person who helps the president with that all-important task of creating more jobs and improving business growth. The department also takes on:

- Gathering the data that tells us whether or not business is happy and healthy in the U.S., and then figuring out what to do about it either way.

- The promotion of U.S. exports and foreign trade.

- Implementing international trade agreements.

- Issuing patents and trademarks.

- Regulating the export of sensitive (read: top-secret) technology and goods.

- Supporting the research and development of technology and engineering.

Department of Labor
Run by: The Secretary of Labor

Black lung? Tough. Four-year-old heavy machinery operator? It's practically cute. Broke your leg on the job? Deal with it.

We haven't always treated the American worker with what you might call respect. But after a couple of centuries of protesting and labor unions and employee deaths, we started to figure it out. These days, the Department of Labor is around to:

- Administer federal labor laws, including those that protect rights to safe and healthy working conditions, minimum wage and overtime pay, a discrimination-free workplace, and unemployment insurance with OSHA—the **Occupational Safety and Health Administration.**

- Research labor conditions in the U.S. today and provide statistics with the **Bureau of Labor Statistics.**

- Administer job training.

- Pay private pensions when employers can't.

- Provide final verdict on worker-protection appeals.

- Fight child labor and trafficking.

- Try to improve job opportunities for people with disabilities.

- Help veterans find good jobs.

- Develop policies to promote women and disadvantaged minority groups in the workplace.

Department of Housing and Urban Development
Run by: The Secretary of Housing and Urban Development

HUD grew out of post–Great Depression and post-war agencies that were designed to help Americans find a reasonably priced place to live—but HUD now seeks to promote "fair and equal housing" across the board by:

- Enforcing federal fair-housing laws.

- Providing mortgage and loan insurance through the Federal Housing Administration.

- Providing rental assistance through Section 8[16] certificates and low-income vouchers.

- Providing government-subsidized housing for low-income families and individuals.

- Providing Community Development Block Grants to help communities improve their economy, job market, and housing.

- Providing homeless assistance funding to local nonprofits.

- Providing funding to improve and replace existing public housing developments.

Department of Transportation
Run by: The Secretary of Transportation

Planes, trains, and automobiles—without the DoT, our roads would crumble into dust, our tracks would rust into oblivion,

---

[16] This is a program that allows private landlords to rent houses and apartments to low-income families at fair market value—the government then subsidizes that rent through a subsidy paid directly to the landlord.

our seas would roil with janky ships, and our skies would become a chaos of flying machines. All right, maybe not quite so dramatic, but you get where we're going here. State and local governments are responsible for a lot of transportation infrastructure, but the DoT:

- Develops, implements, and enforces federal regulations governing roads, highways, airports, air corridors, railways, and seaports.

- Provides federal funding to lower-level government for construction and upkeep of roads and bridges.

- Helps maintain interstate highways.

- Regulates certain safety standards in the auto industry.

- Creates and improves safety regulation for commercial vehicles.

- Serves as the primary oversight agency of the aviation industry with the **Federal Aviation Administration.**

- Develops and enforces railroad safety regulation with the **Federal Railroad Administration.**

- Is responsible for all water transportation and the merchant marines and secures their safety and security with the **Maritime Administration.**

- Keeps us safe when hazardous materials are moved over land, air, or sea in the U.S.

Department of Energy
Run by: The Secretary of Energy

The DoE grew out of the Manhattan Project—our top-secret nuclear stockpile effort—and later, the Atomic Energy Commission.

The Department today is more energy, generally, and less mutually assured destruction. It's around to:

- Develop and promote nuclear power.

- Maintain our nuclear weapons complex (I mean . . . old habits die hard).

- Oversee the cleanup of said nuclear weapons complex (those Cold War-era facilities are just chock-a-block with toxic waste).

- Manage problems left over at said nuclear weapons complex after said cleanup is done.

- Manage nuclear waste disposal sites in the U.S.

- Research and develop alternative and "clean" fuels and promote use of these fuels.

- Market hydropower.

- Oversee electrical, natural gas, and oil industries.

- Explore and develop coal and natural gas energy sources.

- Make sure the electrical grid is working properly.

Department of Veterans Affairs
Run by: The Secretary of Veterans Affairs

During the Civil War, Honest Abe took stock of the ravages of our infighting and called on Congress "to care for him who shall have borne the battle and for his widow, and his orphan." It's the motto of the VA to this day, as an agency tasked with providing the following services to U.S. veterans:

- Education and vocational rehabilitation.

- Pensions, home loans, disability benefits, and life insurance.

- A network of healthcare facilities through the **Veterans Health Administration,** providing medical services in outpatient clinics, hospitals, nursing homes, and outreach centers.

- National cemeteries around the country for the burial of veterans and their family members.

Department of Education
Run by: The Secretary of Education

The smallest of the executive departments, as education is decentralized in the U.S.—we leave the education of our young minds in the hands of state and local officials. The only real way that the department is able to wield power is by dangling a financial carrot in front of states and schools across the country.

The Department of Education supports and guides education in the U.S. by:

- Providing funding for programs[17] that come with a bunch of federal rules that must be met if the schools want the money.

---

[17] There are loads of these programs and they cover a lot of ground. They can be anything from No Child Left Behind, which aims to ensure that all schools, regardless of being in a low-income district, are meeting state academic standards, to IDEA Special Education grants, which provide schools with funding to make sure children with disabilities are properly prepared for higher education.

- Providing loans, grants, and work-study assistance to undergraduate and graduate students.

- Researching and providing grants to aid in the education of children and adults with disabilities.

- Addressing school safety concerns and offering drug and violence-prevention programs.

- Enforcing federal civil rights laws that prohibit discrimination in programs that receive federal funds.

THE INDEPENDENT AGENCIES

In addition to the executive branch departments, there are loads of independent federal agencies in the United States that are considered "executive agencies," but are not headed by someone on the president's Cabinet. Because the term "agency" doesn't have a legal definition at the federal level, it's difficult to say how many federal agencies there actually are. Some of the major ones are as follows.

- **The Federal Trade Commission,** which promotes consumer protection and enforces non-criminal antitrust laws.

- **The Federal Election Commission,** which enforces campaign finance law.

- **The Federal Communications Commission,** which regulates interstate and international radio, television, cable, wire, and satellite communication.

- **The Central Intelligence Agency,** which is the primary human intelligence provider for the federal government. It gathers foreign intelligence and provides policymakers with national security assessments. Also, the director is the only federal government employee who can spend "un-vouchered" money, meaning they don't have to say who they're paying or what they're paying for. So cool. So scary.

- **The Environmental Protection Agency,** which enforces our environmental standards, and has over 14,000 employees.

- **The Securities and Exchange Commission,** which protects investors by regulating stock exchanges and preventing securities fraud.

- **The Small Business Administration,** which watches over small business interests in the U.S., provides small business loans, helps them out in the event of a natural disaster, and helps small businesses get contract work with the federal government.

- **The Social Security Administration,** which administers retirement, disability, and survivors' benefits to the public.

- **The United States Postal Service,** which delivers the mail and operates post offices.

- **The National Labor Relations Board,** which prevents and polices unfair labor practices.

3

THE JUDICIAL BRANCH

The least dangerous branch."

That there is a direct quote from "Federalist No. 78," Alexander Hamilton's essay on the Judicial Branch written in 1788. He also said the judiciary was "next to nothing." And it's no wonder, the Constitution didn't grant it a lot of powers. Article III stipulates that there be a chief justice, but makes no mention of how many other justices serve on the bench.

> **CONSTITUTION 101**: "Article III is so short." "How short is it?" "It's so short that it wasn't allowed on the tilt-a-whirl." But seriously, both Articles II and III are ruthlessly terse, leaving some interpretation to the powers of the president and the Supreme Court. One scholar told us that the reason for this is that the framers had finally finished the all-important powers of Congress, and they wanted to get out of there before Rhode Island showed up and made a mess of everything.

The first Supreme Court, headed by Chief Justice John Jay, had only six justices, a number set by Congress in 1789. During

Jay's tenure and for the following two chief justices, the court heard a paltry fourteen cases. And they had no official meeting place! They knocked around various governmental halls and wings, even spending a stint in the basement below the Senate in 1860.

But this peripatetic crew of robes and opinions, mainly through their own devices, slowly grew into the most powerful judicial body in the world. But first, let's talk about who they are and what they do.

'TIL DEATH DO US PART

Supreme Court justices are appointed by the president with the advice and consent of the Senate through the process we outline in our section on the executive branch. But Supreme Court justice appointments (and all federal judge appointments) are for *life*. They can retire (and they usually do, it's rare for a judge to

die on the bench) or they can be impeached in the House and summarily removed in the Senate.[1] There's no other way. *You* can't vote them out of office. And the Constitution says you can't reduce their salaries during their term, which is ever. So if you don't like the way a justice votes, you'll just have to hope they change their mind someday.

POWERS OF THE SUPREME COURT

The less-sexy powers of the court are that it hears cases involving ambassadors, public officials, and states. Otherwise, most of the time, it is what is called an *appellate court,* which means it hears appeals. A federal case will rise through the court systems until (if the court chooses to take it) it gets a final hearing in the highest chamber in the land.

However, the most important power of the Supreme Court was bestowed upon itself *by* itself in 1803, in the landmark decision of *Marbury v. Madison.* We go into more detail on the specifics of that case in our section *The Robes,* but basically Chief Justice John Marshall wrote that the Supreme Court was not the branch responsible for enforcing the law, but it is the body that decides whether a law or decision made by the government is or is not constitutional. Even if the people and the president and the Congress disagree, the Supreme Court has the final say. This is called **judicial review,** and if it's not on the test then that test isn't worth taking.

---

[1] Most impeachments involve federal judges. As of 2019, fifteen have been impeached, eight of whom were removed from office.

JUDICIAL REVIEW

Our Constitution is the supreme law of the land. And it is *brief.*

> **CONSTITUTION 101:** It's 4,543 words, to be exact; counting the signatures but not the amendments. Only Monaco, Jordan, and Vatican City have shorter ones. India has the longest national constitution at 146,385 words, but that is dwarfed by the state constitution of Alabama, which clocks in at 345,000.

Because of these two factors, it is necessary for there to be a body to interpret the Constitution, to decide what could be law. The power of judicial review, along with the amendment process, makes our constitution a living document that grows with us.

If a party loses a case in the Supreme Court, there is nobody to appeal it to. It is the final arbiter of law in the United States. However, if a law is struck down by a decision, nothing is stopping the legislature from making a different law.[2] Courts and Congress can bat these back and forth all the livelong day.

On some rare occasions (under three hundred, at last count), the Supreme Court will overturn its own decisions. This is when the court hears a different case dealing with the same constitutional issues, and votes the other way due to cultural, political, or technological changes in society. The quintessential example of this is *Brown v. Board of Education,* which ruled racial segregation in schools unconstitutional. Fifty years earlier, the Court in *Plessy*

---

[2] An example of this is the 1989 decision of *Texas v. Johnson,* where the court ruled that burning a U.S. Flag was protected speech. In immediate response to that decision, the 101st Congress passed the "Flag Protection Act of 1989," which the Supreme Court had to strike down the next year.

v. Ferguson had found segregation to be permissible, under the standard of "separate but equal."

HOW A CASE GETS TO THE SUPREME COURT

With difficulty.

Okay, that was a bit flip, but if you have the time and the money for legal counsel, there is nothing stopping you from appealing your case towards the very top. But that last step is a doozy. Because, and we'll get into this later, you have *no right* to have your case heard by the Supreme Court. You have to ask their permission. Every time you hear someone shout in a movie, "I'm gonna take this all the way up to the Supreme Court if I have to!" you now have the right to mutter, "Fat chance."

But clearly some cases do make it up to the top, through two roads. We'll start with the one less traveled.

State Court

About 10 percent of cases that the Supremes hear come through state courts. Which is interesting, because the vast majority of *all* court cases are in state court. If you steal a car, have trouble with an uncle's will, jump a subway turnstile, all that goes to your state court, because someone was violating a *statute,* a law of your state. And it's usually dealt with in your state, there's no reason to make a federal case out of it. But if there's a constitutional question about the statute itself, that's something that can be appealed to a higher court. Each state has its own supreme court, which can appeal directly to the U.S. Supreme Court. But most cases get to the top via . . .

District Court

There are ninety-six federal district courts in the country. Judges in those courts try civil and criminal cases[3] (but mostly civil), and if you lose in that court, you can appeal it up to your circuit court. However . . . when you appeal a case, you are *not* contesting the verdict of the jury. In our system, only the jury can decide facts, so if they decide you're guilty, you're guilty, whether you actually did what you're accused of or not. The only thing you can do on appeal is argue that there was something wrong with the *way* the trial went, or the law itself. Maybe the judge refused a crucial piece of evidence, or jury selection wasn't fair, or maybe the law you've been found guilty of breaking isn't constitutional. That's what you're appealing to the circuit court.

Circuit Court

This goes back to our muddy, carriage-weathered judges in days of yore. The first Supreme Court justices were expected to travel the country to rule on these circuit appeals, and many nearly died in the process. Now, we appoint judges for this, and we have divided the nation (not unlike college basketball) into thirteen circuits. Eleven of those are based on geographic location, one more is in Washington, D.C. The thirteenth circuit is called the Federal Circuit, and it predominantly deals with patent law cases.

---

[3] In case you're wondering about the difference between a civil and a criminal case, civil cases are usually disputes between individuals and/or organizations, and criminal cases are when, well, somebody did something bad. Criminal. Harmful to society. This is why criminal cases are named "State vs." or "The People vs." because the accused violated state law.

The parties in circuit court (and all appellate courts) are not a plaintiff and a defendant, but rather a *petitioner* and a *respondent.* The *petitioner* is the party that lost the case in the lower court, and they are petitioning to have the decision overturned.[4] The *respondent* is the party that won the previous case. Lawyers for each party file a **brief,** a wonderful, succinct document that outlines their legal reasoning, and those briefs are then read by a panel of three circuit court judges.

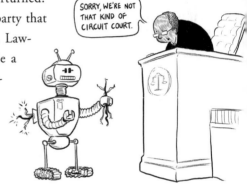

SORRY, WE'RE NOT THAT KIND OF CIRCUIT COURT.

Sometimes this trio of judges makes a decision solely based on the briefs, and sometimes they have a hearing with the attorneys to ask questions. Either way, they deliver one of these decisions:

- **Affirm:** The lower court was right! Why are you wasting everybody's time?

- **Reverse:** Your attorney must have written a hell of a brief, because this means the lower court made the wrong decision and should've found for the other guy.

---

[4] Fun fact, the petitioner always comes first in the name of a case. When you see *Wisconsin v. Yoder,* you know that Wisconsin lost last time and they're not happy about it.

- **Remand:** This is where the appellate court cleans up a few particularities in the case and sends it back to the lower court for a retrial with some specific instructions. It's not uncommon for the circuit court to combine these decisions; you can reverse and remand, meaning the other party should've won, but the retrial can determine how much money should be paid in damages.

And that's *usually* where things end. The circuit court of appeals is immensely powerful, and their decisions are hammered in figurative stone.

GET THAT WRIT

But let's say you're not the type who gives up. What happened to you was *unfair* and those circuit judges were wrong and you're not going to take this lying down. Your only recourse is to file a *petition for a writ of certiorari.*[5] Often referred to as a *cert petition,* this document is the official request to have your case heard in the Supreme Court. A cert petition states the facts of the case and why it's so crucial for the court to hear it. It is *not* a document saying why one party should win versus the other, it's purely the rationale for having it go before the highest court in the land. One of the most common reasons given is what is called a "circuit split," an issue where one circuit has ruled one way and another circuit has done the complete opposite. If an issue is contradicted in several circuits, your case has a much better

---

[5] This is pronounced SER-she-o-RARE-eye. Maybe. Not even the justices agree, honestly.

chance of getting in front of the nine.[6] Because until that split is corrected, the Constitution and federal laws mean different things in different parts of the country.

One other way a case gets to the top is via the office of the **Solicitor General,** the person responsible for representing the United States in the Supreme Court. If they ask the Court to take a case, they'll likely do so.

The Supreme Court reviews these petitions, and if four of the nine justices[7] decide that a case should go before the court, it gets placed on the docket. But the odds aren't in your favor. Of the seven thousand to eight thousand cert petitions that get filed each year, the court agrees to hear about eighty.

> **JUDICIAL BRANCH 101:** There are twenty-eight petition-winnowing meetings of the Supreme Court before hearings begin in October, the most notable of which is called the "Long Conference," where upwards of two thousand petitions are considered. Clerks, who do an unbelievable amount of work for the justices, prepare concise summaries and recommendations, and the nonet select a handful to take to the big show. These cert meetings are not public, and the court's reasoning for not taking certain cases is a well-kept secret.

That's about 0.01 percent. And here is one way that the ideologies of the nine justices can have a quiet but resounding effect

---

[6] One of the most famous recent circuit splits was in the case of *Obergefell v. Hodges,* where the Supreme Court ruled that the Constitution grants same-sex couples the right to marry. The sixth circuit had ruled same-sex marriage bans to be constitutional, whereas the fourth, seventh, ninth, and tenth circuits had found such bans *un*constutional. A national decision had to be made.

[7] This number, four out of nine instead of a simple majority, ensures that a party in the minority still has the power to get a case in front of the court.

on our legal system; whereas a Supreme Court opinion requires deliberation and the justices putting their name on one side or the other, it's far easier to just not touch a sensitive issue.

But let's say your ship comes in. You hear a knock on your door in the middle of the night, and you open it to see a small lad with a stoic countenance. He thrusts a piece of paper into your hand before running off into the rainy darkness. With trembling hands, you hold it to the light and read "CONGRAT-ULATIONS. YOUR CASE IS GOING TO THE SUPREME COURT."[8]

YOUR DAY IN COURT

After a writ has been granted, the petitioner has forty-five days to file *another* brief. This one is called a *merits brief,* and unlike our earlier petition, this time it's all about why they should win. And it's not called a brief for nothing; a merits brief must not exceed fifty pages. Thirty-five days later, the respondent's merits brief is due. Also, and you're probably tired of hearing about briefs at this point but this is the last one, parties who aren't directly involved in a case but have a strong, significant interest in the outcome can file an *amicus brief.*

An argument in the Supreme Court bears little resemblance to courtroom action that we may be familiar with, with a plaintiff and a defendant and a jury and maybe some bongo drums. The petitioner and the respondent often aren't even in the chamber, it's just their lawyers, referred to as advocates.

---

[8] Okay, it doesn't happen like that, the attorneys get a call. But come on, *it's so exciting.*

Beginning at 10 a.m. on that hallowed first Monday in October, the justices are announced as they enter, and the Marshal gives the traditional chant.[9] Then, each case gets about an hour of argument divvied up between the advocates, with the counsel for the petitioner taking the lectern first. As there is no jury, the advocate speaks directly to the justices; giving an opening statement and addressing the justices when they ask questions. One lawyer who once worked in the office of the solicitor general told us that being at the lectern was akin to "sitting in a living room with nine very smart people who have thought about the same problem that you have and want to ask you some questions about it. And your job is to answer them." The petitioner and the respondent each have thirty minutes to speak, and they may reserve some of their time for rebuttal.

At 11 a.m., the advocates from the first case leave and the whole thing starts again. Nowadays the court hears one to two cases on a given day, though there were times in the early 1900s where they'd hear four to five.

THE VOTE

On Wednesdays and Fridays, the court meets for the **Justices' Conference** to vote on the cases heard on the previous two days. Nobody from the public or press is allowed in these conferences,

---

[9] The chant is as follows: "The Honorable, the Chief Justice, and the Associate Justices of the Supreme Court of the United States. Oyez! Oyez! Oyez! All persons having business before the Honorable, the Supreme Court of the United States, are admonished to draw near and give their attention, for the Court is now sitting. God save the United States and this Honorable Court!" The word "oyez" comes from the plural imperative form of "ouïr" (to hear) in French, and basically means "listen up!"

neither are any clerks or other employees of the court, it is just the nine justices. The most junior associate justice is tasked with guarding the door and requesting outside materials.[10] In a time-honored tradition, they all shake hands before the conference begins. When discussing each case, the chief justice speaks first, then each justice in descending order of seniority. Nobody interrupts during these statements. Finally, they all vote.

The justices in the majority are tasked with writing the opinion, and those in the minority can (if they wish) write the dissenting opinion. Sometimes justices agree with the majority but have different legal reasoning for doing so, in which case they can write a concurring opinion. And each justice may write their individual dissenting opinions. Each justice can change their vote based on these opinions, so the opinions and dissents undergo many rewrites in an attempt to sway more votes to either side.

THAT'S JUST YOUR OPINION, MAN

While the court knows how they're going to vote pretty soon after hearing cases, the official announcement isn't made public until the opinion is written, and that can take *months*. The deadline for all opinions is late June to early July, and the last few weeks of the session (before the summer break) are devoted entirely to the court delivering their opinions. Each decision contains the following parts:

- **Syllabus:** This is a summary of the facts of the case and how the court rules. It's short, snappy, and it details how each justice voted.

---

[10] And making coffee. Seriously.

- **Main Opinion:** This is the meat of a Supreme Court decision, and a majority of justices have to sign on that they agree with it. These can be many pages, outlining the legal reasoning and precedent for voting the way they did.

- **Concurring and Dissenting Opinions:** The best part. Always fun to read. Impassioned arguments on why a justice's colleagues are dead wrong. Sometimes, in cases like *Scott v. Sanford* or *Plessy v. Ferguson,* dissents are prophetic; prequels to a court reversal further down the line.

- **Disposition:** This is the action the court is taking, just like in the circuit court—affirm, reverse, or remand.

NOW WHAT?

Here's the snarly, sometimes frustrating truth about the Supreme Court. Yes, these decisions are footnotes to the Constitution. And yes, the power of the judiciary has grown from "next to nothing" to the final arbiter of American law. But after a decision is read, after the cheering and the sobbing and the headlines, we enter the labyrinth of applying that ruling. Let's end with an example.

In the decision of *Loving v. Virginia* in 1967, the court unanimously voted that a Virginia law preventing interracial marriage was unconstitutional. Chief Justice Earl Warren said, "the freedom to marry, or not marry, a person of another race resides with the individual, and cannot be infringed by the State." This meant each state with laws forbidding or punishing interracial marriage had to remove them. However, Virginia didn't change that law for another year. West Virginia, Florida, Oklahoma, and Missouri did in 1969. North Carolina, a year after that. Georgia, Louisiana, and Mississippi finally did so in 1972, and Delaware and Kentucky in 1974. Tennessee had race-based marriage restrictions until 1978, South Carolina until *1998*.

And finally, in the year 2000, Alabama became the last state to remove its ban on interracial marriage.

Why? How could a very specific, very clear instruction from the Supreme Court take over thirty years to apply to the states? That princess is in another castle. A castle with a moat and a portcullis and a labyrinth, at the center of which lives a uniquely American minotaur called "federalism."

STATES OF THE
UNION

4

FEDERALISM

AMERICA'S ETERNAL TUG-OF-WAR

This is a country of a big, imposing federal government and small, mighty states. Both are in charge of you, both want control, and both are willing to mess with the other to get it. The federal government has a fat wallet and sits around talking to other countries, waging wars, and telling people what to do. States want what's in that wallet, so they begrudgingly behave and keep your little world spinning while they're at it.

This is called federalism.[1] Overarching rules, regulations, and funding that hang heavy over fifty little unsovereign sovereignties. There's a reason we're called the *United States of*

---

[1] If you're thinking, "*federalism*, huh? That makes it sound like the federal government and *only* the federal government is in charge." Well, we're with ya, partner, it sure does. If you ask us, it should be called something like "Simultaneous Compromise-Heavy Governance" or "Ambiguous State-Federal Hierarchical Rule" or "Co-Parenting." But nobody did ask us. So here we are.

America. It's kind of a long title if compared to, say, "Japan."
E pluribus unum.[2] Out of many, one.

A union between independent states
and the federal government. It's kind of
lovely when you think about it.
And then you think harder and
you're like, "but that's crazy!"

HOW AND WHY WE GOT HERE

There are three major governing systems on this strange blue marble, and
our nation has experienced them all.
You've got your basic unitary system
(think England, France, China) where

a big central government holds all the
power, and whatever lower systems of
government exist are there to serve the
will of the people in charge. Then
there's the confederate system,
wherein sovereign states
with loads of autonomy
operate under a central
government with limited
power. I'd name a few

NOT EVEN I,
HERCULE POIROT,
CAN SOLVE THE
MYSTERY OF THE
BELGIAN CONFEDERATE
SYSTEM.

---

[2] *"E Pluribus Unum,"* which appears on the Great Seal of the United States, on
that yellow ribbon that the eagle is holding in its mouth (also, whaaa?), was the de
facto motto of the United States until 1956 when Congress decided to bring the
Big Guy into the mix and passed a joint resolution to make our official motto "In
God We Trust."

but, shocker, these tend not to last very long. It's basically just Belgium.

And then, of course, there's your federal system—a mix of national and smaller governments where power is distributed in the hands of both.

We started off unitary under Mother England, went confederate[3] after we declared independence (no relation to the southern *confederacy*) and finally landed on nice, warm, fraught federalism after hammering it out in Philly in 1787.

You won't find the word "federalism" anywhere in the text of our venerable Constitution, but this theory is scattered throughout it in the explicit and implicit divvying up of federal and state powers. From 1788 and our founding to 1937 and FDR blowin' everything up, the country operated under what we call dual federalism. This was the result of a narrow interpretation of federal versus state powers in the Constitution. It pretty much went like this: the federal government only has jurisdiction if the Constitution explicitly says so. Everything else is up to the states. And that's the Tenth Amendment, folks.

CONSTITUTION 101: The very first line (post-preamble) in the Constitution gives us two definitions. Article I, Section 1 tells us what Congress can *do,* and it tells us what Congress *is,* "All

---

[3] During this pre-Constitution time, we were governed by the Articles of Confederation and Perpetual Union. There was just one branch of government, Congress, and it couldn't levy taxes, regulate commerce, or enforce laws. The United States called itself a "firm league of friendship" and none of those friends wanted to pick up the bill for the Revolutionary War. Despite their fear of a strong central government, the framers had to admit that at the very least a *stronger* central government was in order. So they got together to fix the Articles, realized no way no how was that gonna happen, and ended up writing our Constitution instead.

legislative Powers herein granted shall be vested in a Congress of the United States, which shall consist of a Senate and House of Representatives." What is Congress? It's a Senate and a House. What can it do? Well, if we're interpreting this in a very limited way, it can do what it's been granted to do in the Constitution. Anything else? The Tenth Amendment kinda clears that question up. *"The powers not delegated to the United States by the Constitution, nor prohibited by it to the states, are reserved to the states respectively, or to the people."* So, Congress can only do what the Constitution says it can, and everything else that can be done will be done by the states. This nice, neat version of federalism is gonna change, of course, because we have a nation-changing Civil War to wage and a Great Depression to cut us down to size. But for now, here in our nation's infancy and toddlerhood, we're taking the Constitution pretty literally.

This made the federal government powerful, but limited. It basically meant that the federal government was in charge of foreign affairs, the military, money, and interstate commerce because that's all that's actually enumerated in the Constitution.

AMERICAN FEDERALISM PHASE 1: DUAL FEDERALISM

This is also called Layer Cake Federalism—distinct areas of responsibility and governance that rarely overlap—but we just can't *stand* that cake metaphor, so that's all we'll say about that.

WHAT THE FEDERAL GOVERNMENT COULD DO

Let's start with that money power, shall we? 'Cause, get real, no foreign nation's gonna talk to you or fight with you unless there's money involved. In 1787, we were in loads of debt to France, Spain, and some fancy Dutch private investors. The federal government didn't have the power to levy taxes under the Articles of Confederation (AoC), and so good luck extracting money from citizens to pay off the freedom they won from the planet's most powerful empire.

Enter Article I, Section 8, Clause 1: The Spending Clause. A.k.a., The Federal Government Can Now Levy Taxes, So Everybody Just Be Cool, Okay?

> **CONSTITUTION 101:** The Tenth Amendment says that Congress can impose taxes to pay for three things—debt, protection, and general welfare. These days, that pretty much means that Congress can use taxes to pay for everything.

If we think of the Tenth Amendment as the guiding principle for dual federalism, we can look at the rest of Section 8 as those major powers enumerated. So, in addition to giving Congress the power to levy taxes, Section 8 throws the federal government a bunch of other big ol' bones. Congress is given the power to:

* Borrow money from other countries.
* Regulate commerce.
* Coin money and regulate its value.
* Punish counterfeiters.
* Establish post offices.

* Establish roads.

* Manage patents.

* Punish pirates (yup).

* Declare war.

* Raise armies.

* Suppress insurrection and repel invasion.

WHAT THE STATES HAD TO DO

While the federal government had control over some big-ticket items, states enjoyed the catchall "you get everything else" of the Tenth Amendment. Under this dual federalism system, states were given the freedom to take care of their own affairs for the most part without the federal government mucking around in them.

The relatively puny Article Four of the Constitution is otherwise known as the States Article. It's here that we find the very few rules and regulations that the Constitution explicitly imposes on the states—it's about the way that states interact with each other and the way that they interact with the federal government.

There's not *much* that the Constitution dictates to the states, and most of it has to do with keeping the peace across state lines. The aim was to keep the United States united, so it's a whole lotta "now, play nice." That's how we ended up with the Full Faith and Credit Clause, for example. It mandates that one state accept the judgment of another state's courts. This idea had been around since the AoC, and the basic idea was to make sure that debtors in one state couldn't make off to another state scot-free. We suppose we could call this the "an American always repays their debts" clause.

The Comity, or Privileges and Immunity, Clause, comes next. Comity basically means a friendly, courteous vibe. No punches below the belt, kids. States aren't allowed to discriminate against the citizens of another state, and they have to respect what happens in another state. This one works in theory, but come on.

Article Four also stipulates that if a convicted felon skips town (or in this case, state), his new hosts have to return him from whence he came. This extended to persons "held in service or labor." If you're thinking that's a coy way of saying escaped enslaved people had to be returned to the people who owned them if they crossed a state line, you would be right. The framers weren't super comfortable discussing slavery. Shocker. These days we refer to this as the Fugitive Slave Clause. It was eliminated with the passing of the Thirteenth Amendment, which abolished slavery.

Under Section 3 of this article, states also couldn't go willy-nilly and admit another state into the union of their own accord, or team up with another state to make some kind of superstate without Congress's go-ahead. It's here where Congress asserts its authority over other territory and property belonging to the U.S.—Arkansas couldn't look westward and decide that it was going to make the rules for the unsettled wild yonder.

Article Four ties everything up with a pretty little promise: It guarantees a republican government to every state in the country. This means that we all get to live in a state run by a representative democracy as opposed to, say, a monarchy. Wanna be King of Florida? Tough noogies. Otherwise known as the Guarantee Clause, it throws in federal protection from invasion and domestic violence, like riots and unrest, at no extra cost!

There you have it. A nice, neat lemon-chiffon-and-mascarpone layer cake of dual-federalism government (darn it, we promised ourselves we wouldn't get cake-y with this one). That mascarpone

stays in its layer and that lemon chiffon stays in *its,* and never the twain shall mush together into one, albeit delicious, mess of governance and interference.

Of course, dual federalism is a *theory* of Constitutional interpretation. It's an *idea.* It's the lemon cake sitting untouched in layers of perfect harmony under a glass cake dome on the counter. But, as we all know, the cake can't stay that way. That mascarpone's going to melt.

THE LIFE AND DEATH OF DUAL FEDERALISM

We don't operate under the theory of dual federalism anymore. There's a cooperative marble cake on the horizon. But it took decades of conflict and Supreme Court cases to finally break us of this commitment to distinct and separate governments. Debates about the constitutionality of federal interference with states' rights went on among the men who actually *wrote* the dang Constitution. How meta is that?

Let's take a stroll through the clashes of state and federal government that eventually gave way to a new theory of federalism altogether. It's a hundred-year tug-of-war between federal and state governments that eventually broke the system wide open.

We begin in 1790 with first-ever secretary of the treasury, Alexander Hamilton. The Constitution is newly ratified, the framers are dreaming big about the myriad possibilities of this new government, and Hamilton asserts himself as quite partial to a strong, centralized federal government. He proposes a national bank, mint, and federal excise tax. Moderate Federalist Thomas Jefferson and staunch Anti-Federalist James Madison argue that the bank is opposed to both the spirit and the letter of the Constitution. Hamilton argues back, gets his way, and George Washington signs the "bank bill" into law.

Eight years later, Congress passes the Alien and Sedition Acts. These are four laws shot from the hip when the Federalist Congress feared war with France was imminent. They make it harder to become a citizen of the United States, give the president the power to imprison and deport noncitizens, and make it illegal to make false statements criticizing the federal government. So yes, it is passed in fear of the French, but these Acts are also meant to stifle Democratic-Republicans—they explicitly make it illegal to criticize Federalists holding high offices, but not illegal to criticize opponents of the Federalists. They are also just straight-up bigoted, as is evidenced by Congressman Harrison Grey Otis's imploring that we not "invite hordes of Wild Irishmen, nor the turbulent and disorderly of all the world, to come here with a basic view to distract our tranquility." Immediately after their passage, Kentucky and Virginia legislatures release resolutions declaring the Alien and Sedition Acts unconstitutional. They also argue that states have the right and duty to declare Congressional acts unconstitutional if the act is not somehow authorized by the Constitution. If a state determines an act to be unconstitutional, the resolutions argue, that state then has the right to nullify the act. George Washington is horrified by these resolutions and fears that, if acted on, they could dissolve the union.

By 1814, the Second Bank of the United States (the first one kinda lapsed) has driven the country into economic depression by way of strict credit policies. Several states oppose the bank and impose taxes on the operation of local branches. James

McCulloch of Maryland's branch refuses to pay the tax, the state sues, and the whole thing gets appealed up to the Supreme Court. Chief Justice John Marshall rules that the bank is constitutional, that the state taxes on the bank are unconstitutional, and establishes the notion of the implied Congressional powers in the Constitution. States freak out over what amounts to the potential for the federal government to assert unlimited powers.

Tensions begin to mount between the industrialized North and agrarian South when, in 1828, Congress passes a tariff on goods imported from Europe that helps to strengthen the North's economy but just makes the southern states furious about having to pay more for European goods. The South, in what could be seen as an early indication of its penchant for lush writing, calls this the Tariff of *Abominations* and declares it unconstitutional for favoring one American economy over another. Four years later, Congress passes another tariff reducing the tariff of the Tariff of Abominations, and with that, the term "tariff" loses all meaning by way of overuse. South Carolina isn't content with the reduction, and declares the tariffs of 1828 and 1832 null and void within the boundary of the state. The Ordinance of Nullification is referred to today as the Nullification Crisis.

Andrew Jackson says that South Carolina's nullification ordinance is pretty much treason and prepares to take military action against the state. Congress passes the Force Act, which basically says that, sure, the president can do that in order to force South Carolina to comply with the tariff. Just as everything is about to blow up, Senators Henry Clay and John C. Calhoun (who was a seriously *wild*-looking dude!) propose the Compromise Tariff to reduce existing tariff rates. South Carolina is cool with this and everybody stands down.

But not for long! By 1850, southern states begin calls for secession. Fearing for the Union, Congress passes a group of five bills designed to placate the South and ease North-South tension over land acquired in the Mexican-American War. The Compromise of 1850, among other provisions, restrengthens the Fugitive Slave Clause with a new Fugitive Slave Act that essentially forces states to aid in the return of fugitive enslaved people. In defiance, Vermont passes a law that requires officials to aid escaped enslaved people. Wisconsin would go on to become the only state to declare the 1850 Fugitive Slave Act unconstitutional.

Dred Scott, an enslaved man, is taken into a territory where slavery is forbidden in 1857. He sues for his freedom, the case is appealed to the Supreme Court, and in an act of abject hideousness, Chief Justice Roger B. Taney rules that Congress does not have the power to prohibit slavery in the territories of the United States. He also rules that Black individuals cannot be citizens of the United States.

Here's the breaking point, folks. This is an instance of executive versus Congress rather than state versus federal government, but it is essential to the downfall of dual federalism. In 1861, Abraham Lincoln issues a public declaration that there is insurrection in the United States and calls for troops to subdue the rebellion. In other words, Lincoln does something that only Congress can do. He starts a war, inventing executive war powers. He then suspends habeas corpus before Congress comes into session. Chief Justice Taney, in *Ex Parte Merryman,* rules that the president cannot do this, nor can he authorize a military office to do this. Lincoln *does not comply*—ooh, things are heating up in here—citing the Constitution, which provides for suspension of the writ.[4] Taney says only Congress can suspend it, but Lincoln controls the military, so. Sorry, Taney. Two years later, Lincoln issues the Emancipation Proclamation.

Three years and 620,000 deaths later, the Civil War ends. Then, in 1868, the groundbreaking Fourteenth Amendment is ratified and the due process and equal protection clause strengthens federal judiciary powers. The amendment nullifies the Dred Scott decision with a broad definition of citizenship that does not exclude formerly enslaved people or their descendants and prevents states from passing laws that deprive any citizens of privileges or immunities. It is designed to protect newly freed enslaved people from the actions of individual states, but it also gives Congress the ability to enforce its provisions. The Fourteenth Amendment requires the states, and not the federal government, to do certain things and significantly expands the power of the federal government to regulate what

---

[4] This is, notably, in Section 1 of the Constitution, meaning it is a power of *Congress* and not of the president.

goes on in the states. Once we start thinking of businesses as "people," by the way, this means Congress can have a say in what a business does.

Continuing the theme of federal control, Congress passes the Comstock Laws in 1873. These make it illegal to send "obscene," "lewd," "lascivious," "immoral," or "indecent" materials through the mail and a misdemeanor to sell, give away, or possess "obscene" materials. "Obscene" is not defined in the law, but it does make explicit that possession of materials on abortion and contraception is illegal. Anthony Comstock, the man who lobbied for the law, is made an agent of the Post Office and empowered to enforce the law, which he does with vigor. Many private citizens are arrested under this law, especially doctors providing materials on birth control.

In 1890, Congress gets all up in our business(es) again with the Sherman Anti-Trust Act. This act outlaws "trusts," a.k.a. monopolies, in order to increase economic competitiveness in the U.S. and paves the way for Congress to keep on keepin' on and pass more acts to regulate business.

In the last gasps of dual federalism, in 1896, the Supreme Court grants rights to some mean and nasty states when it rules in *Plessy v. Ferguson* that segregated facilities, so long as they are "equal," are not in violation of the Fourteenth Amendment's equal protection clause. Then, in *Williams v. Mississippi*, SCOTUS[5] rules that literacy tests (used to determine

---

[5] Again, that acronym stands for Supreme Court of the United States. And for a little fun side trivia, "acronyms" have to be pronounceable (SNAFU, RADAR, etc.) and if they're not (WWF, ROFLMAO), they're "initialisms."

eligibility to vote and discriminate against Black Americans) are permissible.

This tense tug of war, this form of federalism that rode out a civil war that nearly rent the nation asunder, finally takes its last gasping breaths with the election of Teddy Roosevelt, strapping, mustachioed statesman that he is, in 1901. Teddy looks out over this dual federalist country, adjusts his pince-nez, and ushers in the Progressive Era and the groundwork for a new federalism. National interests, he says, have become decentralized. Under this system, we all want so many different things. Look at us! Who even *are* we anymore? Let's come together, Teddy says. Let's protect the common man by way of a strong federal government. Let's have a New Nationalism.

AMERICAN FEDERALISM PHASE 2: ENTR'ACTE

Here we are in a funny little period where, despite a strong government waiting in the wings, the U.S. can still be said to operate under a dual federalist system. The Supreme Court has continued to behave according to the principles of a fixed set of constitutional powers, with the enumerated powers of the federal government limited by those reserved to the states. With the proactive protection of individual liberty in the Fourteenth Amendment, SCOTUS, inadvertently or not, created the perfect environment for the rise of industrialization. American business boomed, deafeningly. But with that boom came the need for some cooperative legislating between federal and state government.

It is under Theodore Roosevelt that the shimmer of intergovernmental cooperation begins. And so we can think of this period as having one foot in dual and the other in cooperative federalism. And sure, if it helps, this is the moment in American federalism where we've got one foot squishing around in the lemon mascarpone and another mashing up the marble cake.

Teddy Roosevelt grew up a sickly child who ran, jumped, and swam his way into an all-American picture of health and robustness. He applied the same purposefulness and rigor to the nation when he assumed the presidency in 1901.

His assumption, by the way, was incidental. Teddy was a young cowboy of a politician who got the job only because William McKinley was shot and killed. In fact, party bosses had elected to stick Roosevelt in the impotent VP role in order to keep him subdued, never suspecting that they'd lose McKinley. The new, young president had on his hands an America where industry had all but been given free rein, where a full half of the population lived in cities, where immigrants had swelled our numbers exponentially and provided the workforce that would make mere businessmen into titans of industry. The *Rockefellers* became a thing at this time, you get me? Corruption ran amok in politics, government, and business. Things were loud and hot and fast and dangerous and dark and slimy.

You know what can stop dangerous, dark, and slimy? The fisticuffs of federal regulation.

When Teddy became president, he operated under an unprecedented assumption—that executive power was

limited only by, and not *to,* the specific restrictions outlined in the Constitution. In other words, before Teddy, presidential powers not granted were forbidden. After Teddy, presidential powers not forbidden were granted. He coined the term "bully[6] pulpit," and used his influence to persuade Congress into a monumental expansion of federal power.

Arguing that the American everyman was owed a "square deal," Teddy broke up massively powerful conglomerates, regulated the railroad system, established national parks in order to preserve the nation for generations to come, and implemented policies to keep food and drugs safe for the American consumer.

EXECUTIVE BRANCH 101: The Sherman Anti-Trust Act was passed under Benjamin Henry Harrison and was designed to regulate and sustain competition in business and prevent the artificial raising of prices. The Act allows the Department of Justice to bring lawsuits against trusts that violate the Act, and Theodore Roosevelt used this provision more than any of his predecessors to break up the bad trusts in America at that time. Now, it was up to Teddy to determine what was a "bad" trust and he was much less likely to set his sights on you if you were a buddy of his. Was it legal for the president to go around busting trusts (and inconsistently at that)? As a Progressive, Teddy Roosevelt believed it was the job of the government to make things fair between powerful interests and the common man. If trust busting accomplished that, he figured, it was legal.

Teddy also argued that the worker ought to be protected, leading to the establishment of the Department of Labor and

---

[6] The good kind of bully! The "bully for you!" kind of bully, meaning excellent, wonderful, huzzah!

Commerce, new labor laws, and the eventual end of child labor.

Teddy Roosevelt was criticized for his vigorous use of executive power, but what did he care? He gazed out over a United States regulated and reformed and believed he had played his rightful role in the country he helped to govern. Teddy's autobiography was published in 1913,[7] a year after he lost a presidential bid to Woodrow Wilson. In it, he sums up what his presidency *did* to the presidency. By sheer force of will, Theodore Roosevelt created the executive branch anew. He wrote:

"My view was that every executive officer, and above all every executive officer in high position, was a steward of the people, and not content himself with the negative merit of keeping his talents undamaged in a napkin. I declined to adopt the view that what was imperatively necessary for the nation could not be done by the president unless he could find some specific authorization to do it. My belief was that it was not only his right but his duty to do anything that the needs of the nation demanded unless such action was forbidden by the Constitution or by the laws. Under this interpretation of executive power I did and caused to be done many things not previously done by the president and

---

[7] This also happens to be the year that Teddy helped lead a survey expedition along the Rio de Duvida (the "River of Doubt"), later renamed the Rio Roosevelt. The expedition was plagued by bad luck the whole time—nineteen men embarked, only sixteen returned, and Roosevelt himself nearly died from infection after receiving a gash in his leg. Roosevelt's son, Kermit, did not want to join the expedition as he'd just gotten engaged, but his mother, Edith, insisted he go to protect his dad. Teddy never fully recovered, and though he considered a 1920 presidential bid, he died in 1919 before he could give it another go. I mean. You can't make this stuff up, the dude was wild.

the heads of the departments. I did not usurp power, but I did greatly broaden the use of executive power."

Remember, federalism is a theory that we use to interpret the U.S. Constitution. Teddy Roosevelt boldly decided to apply an entirely different interpretive theory, but it wouldn't be given a proper name for another couple of decades. The five presidents who followed Teddy enjoyed a new position at the center of American politics as dual federalism slowly died out. In this period, the national government continued Teddy's notion of stewardship-plus—sure, the government was the servant to the states but maybe the servant had some pretty firm ideas about what the states needed.

Woodrow Wilson established his New Freedom program, designed to support small farms and businesses with tariff and banking reform. The Sixteenth Amendment established a federal income tax. The federal government established a number of land grants to support state government programs. The line between state and federal started to get fuzzy as the tendrils of federal money and power reached into the states.

It wasn't until another Roosevelt took office, however, that the executive power would once again be so forcefully wielded, and a new theory of federalism firmly established.

AMERICAN FEDERALISM PHASE 3: COOPERATIVE FEDERALISM

When Franklin Delano Roosevelt took office in 1933, the country was a *disaster.* The stock market had crashed four years earlier, and we were a little less than halfway through the Great Depression. Unemployment, poverty, deflation, a freakin' dust bowl, for the love of *mike*, we were in bad shape. The country had become a mewling, peevish creature in need of some strong guidance. A square deal wouldn't be enough. We'd need a deal that was entirely new.

The New Deal

Empowered by Congress in this era of national devastation, FDR used the federal government to attempt to fix the country. During his first 105 days, the president and his team got fifteen major bills through a Congress that essentially said yes to their every request.[8] They enacted a sweeping farm relief bill and large-scale welfare and public works programs. States

---

[8] But the Supreme Court said no! Many of FDR's New Deal laws were initially ruled unconstitutional and struck down by SCOTUS. So FDR proposes that justices either retire at seventy or get assigned a presidentially appointed "assistant," which would effectively stack the court with as many as six more justices handpicked by Roosevelt. The proposal was lambasted by much of Congress and it's unlikely that a court-stacking plan would've been passed by Congress, *but* before the bill could even come before our legislature, two justices ruled in favor of the Social Security Act and the National Labor Relations Act. With the court behind his New Deal legislation, FDR stood down. This change of heart is referred to today as the "switch in time that saved nine."

immediately started receiving millions of dollars from the federal government. Just to put people to work, Roosevelt established the CCC—Civilian Conservation Corps—and hired a quarter million people to fix the disrepair of the national parks that his distant cousin Teddy had created. FDR went so far as to request, and receive, federal regulation of the stock market.

> **EXECUTIVE BRANCH 101:** This is, in fact, why we put so much emphasis on a president's first hundred days in office. After the spectacular show by FDR, subsequent presidents would be scrutinized for their first three months. Basically, FDR created a new America, what're *you* gonna do?

Over the course of his *long* presidency, FDR's administration oversaw the creation of our modern welfare and regulatory states. He established Social Security and unemployment insurance; created the Securities and Exchange Commission; created a federal minimum wage; and created the National Labor Relations Board. He created an America in which lower- and middle-class workers were protected from the top down and the banks had to answer to the federal government. Under this New Deal coalition,[9] FDR solidified a new federalism: cooperative federalism.

> **CONSTITUTION 101:** FDR changed the country, and the presidency, in many ways—including the triggering of a constitutional amendment. Roosevelt was the first and only president to serve more than two terms. He earned the nickname "the Sphinx" as he was nearing the end of his second term and

---

[9] The New Deal coalition was not an official organization, but instead refers to the voting blocs and interest groups that voted for Democratic presidential candidates beginning in 1932.

refused to tell the media if he'd be going for a third. Go for a third he did. And a fourth. FDR was president from 1933 to his death, in office, in 1945. FDR is considered to be one of our greatest presidents, up there with Washington and Lincoln, but people also thought his approach smacked of dictatorship. The Twenty-Second Amendment was passed two years after Roosevelt's death and ratified by the states in 1951. It limits a person to two terms in the presidency, or up to eight years if they assume the presidency following the death of the sitting president, then run and repeatedly win.

Sharing the Power

Here's the marble cake. The swirly, whirly all-mixed-up-in-each-other's-business cake. Agencies at the state and federal levels share power and carry out programs together. Because the national government has become involved in education, health, and welfare, it means there is some consistency from state to state in terms of services provided. Federal statutes are established, and states are either given the leeway to implement these statutes in the bounds of federal regulation, or federal regulation preempts state law.

Programs like Medicaid and Aid to Families with Dependent Children are established at the federal level and implemented at the state. Social Security and Medicaid come directly from the

federal government, but each state is required to have a coordinator for the program.

It may seem, then, that the states are bound entirely to the will of the federal government. But, in fact, the federal government relies almost entirely on the states to implement policy and the states are reserved an immense amount of discretion in that implementation. Under cooperative federalism, the federal government comes up with the big, mushy idea and the state governments mold that mush into practical application.

For decades, this is the federalism that ruled supreme. There are those who say this is the federalism that *continues* to rule, limiting us to those two cakes. The lemon mascarpone layers of the past and the chocolate-vanilla marble cake of today. But what if, *what if,* there's a third cake?

That's right, we said it! If we're going to use this stupid metaphor, then we're going to lean all the way in.

Social reform and programs continued to be doled out at the federal level through the Civil Rights Era and Lyndon Johnson's "Great Society." Johnson actually called this "creative federalism," and it lasted throughout the '50s and '60s. But the '70s was a wild time, man. I mean, the energy crisis? The Iran hostage crisis? The *Watergate* crisis?

EXECUTIVE BRANCH 101: Lyndon B. Johnson sought to totally eliminate poverty and racial injustice. You know, the easy stuff. He signed the Civil Rights Act of 1964, the Voting Rights Act of 1965, and the Elementary and Secondary Education Act of 1965. He launched his "War on Poverty" and created an Office of Economic Opportunity, launched loads of programs such as the Model Cities Program for urban development and

> Upward Bound for impoverished high school students entering college. Johnson even authorized Medicaid and Medicare and created the National Endowments for the Arts and Humanities.

And all of this a prologue to Reagan and a whole different federalism altogether.

AMERICAN FEDERAL PHASE 4: NEW FEDERALISM

See, Lyndon Johnson's legislative pushes were on par with FDR's in scope and number. He did a lot of *stuff*. He managed to establish a slate of social programs that remain crucial to society to this day. He also managed to alienate social and fiscal conservatives the nation over and ended his presidency hated by many. Nixon took over and started to roll things back a bit. He took many of the categorical grants[10] being offered to states for various programs and consolidated them into block grants.[11] This put a little power back in the hands of the states. Then, in 1976, the

---

[10] Funding provided to state and local government for a specific designated purpose.

[11] Funding provided to state and local governments that can be used for any purpose.

Supreme Court ruled in favor of state sovereignty in the seminal *National League of Cities v. Usery* case.

Things were starting to heat up. Finally, after a dab of Ford and a smattering of Carter, Reagan stepped into office and took up the welfare gauntlet. Or rather, put it down.

Reagan wanted the federal government to spend less on state social programs. Not cut 'em off completely, just wean them a bit. He oversaw a reduction in the size and scope of federal grants of about 25 percent, forcing states to step it up when it came to the oversight and funding of social programs. Reagan wasn't shy about it—he saw this as the proper implementation of federalism. In fact, he wrote an executive order about it. Executive Order 12612: Federalism. *We kid you not.*

The purpose of this order was to "restore the division of governmental responsibilities between the national government and the states that was intended by the framers of the Constitution and to ensure that the principles of federalism established by the framers guide the executive departments and agencies in the formulation and implementation of policies."

In other words, gimme a layered marble cake, stat.

It wasn't so much a call to return to the dual federalism of our founding as it was a call for better balance between state and federal government. One where federal government maintains its supremacy, but state governments accept greater responsibility for social and economic programs. It was called the "devolution revolution."

Still, the Supreme Court is where the federalism meets the road, and it continued to operate along a somewhat disempowered Tenth Amendment line for a long while after Reagan put in his order at the cake bakery. In fact, it wasn't until 1995 and the case of the *United States v. Lopez* that things started to shift. This was the first case since 1937 in which SCOTUS ruled that Congress had exceeded its power to legislate under the Commerce Clause. Five years later, SCOTUS would rule in *United States v. Morrison* that parts of the Violence Against Women Act were unconstitutional in that they exceeded powers granted by the Commerce and Equal Protection Clauses.

> **JUDICIAL BRANCH 101:** In *US v. Lopez*, a San Antonio high school student challenged the Gun-Free School Zones Act of 1990, and the court ruled that Congress did not, in fact, have the power to regulate the carrying of handguns under the Commerce Clause.

So what does this mean? Is SCOTUS on a states' rights binge? Is Congress losing its grip on Supremacy? Are we staring down the barrel of another new federalism? An old federalism? Is this Reagan's world or are we in different territory altogether?

AMERICAN FEDERALISM PHASE 5: EVERYTHING AT ONCE

In the over two centuries since our constitution was written, federalism has shifted based on what the nation demanded at the time.

When we were fresh off our breakup with Britain, smarting from the failed Articles of Confederation but too burnt from the motherland to accept a particularly strong national government, our federalism reflected that. Separate and clearly enumerated powers.

As we expanded west, as business boomed and wars waged, the executive branch decided it was time for some ground rules. In order to protect not just the nation as a whole but the rights of the individual, we transitioned into a federalism that allowed the government to act as more of a warden to businesses and citizens.

But that's a lot of work. A lot of work and a lot of taxes. Big government was no match for the country-factioning of the Vietnam War, brutal race riots, and the civil rights movement. It was a nation drunk on that wild cocktail that elected Richard Nixon and ushered in an era of budget cuts and tax wariness. And then Nixon *really* brought the house down with the Watergate scandal, casting the populace into some major doubt as far as the feds go.

Reagan's "devolution revolution" and new federalism kicked off an era that handed lots of power back to the states. But the federal government continued to grow in authority as well. We're now at a time when federalism is defined by debates about abortion, marijuana, police, and guns. The federal government says it is a crime to possess, buy, or sell marijuana, but the drug is being sold "legally" in regulated dispensaries across the country. The Supreme Court has ruled unconstitutional any laws that put an undue burden on a woman's right to an abortion before viability, yet restrictive abortion bans have been cropping up in states across the country.

The country has been polarized ever since the Reagan-Bush era, and a firm ideological divide means that state and local government is being looked to more and more for finely tailored legislation. When the president or federal Congressional majority strong-arms a law that the minority party considers reprehensible (Obamacare, say, or a travel ban on predominantly Muslim countries), minority-controlled states can, and do, sue the federal government. They're doing it in record numbers these days.[12]

This is the federalism of political divide and litigiousness. It's a federalism where the government is big and powerful and passing divisive laws, and states sue. Contained in today's federalism are the applications of all past phases as well. There's the assertion of states' rights, and the protection of specifically those citizens therein, of dual federalism. There's the big government imposition of cooperative and creative federalism. The block grants and federal power divestment of new federalism reign supreme in state budget and regulatory decisions. And all the while, we're making use of the great mediator—the courts—in order to keep this precarious plate spinning.

When we chose to have a constitutional republic, we were acquiescing to something sticky. Not unlike the cake stand after you've finally finished that thing off. We agreed to essentially be at amicable odds forever. Or for as long as we could

---

[12] The Obama administration was involved in 46 multistate lawsuits (suits where state attorneys general team up), and Trump's suits have since outpaced that. Presidential administrations have not faced multistate suits on this scale since Reagan, and he capped out at 39.

manage to keep it up. Through depression, recession, war, rioting, impeachment—it's a system that can take what you throw at it. There will always be a new version of federalism because we just can't sit still around here, and the division of power sways accordingly. Though we've yet to name this modern era of federalism ("judicial federalism" is being thrown around), the principles we establish now will appear in our future methods of governing ourselves. Federalism is iterative.

So, when you get down to it, federalism isn't a cake at all. It's a turducken.[13]

---

[13] A monstrous dish consisting of a deboned chicken stuffed inside of a deboned duck stuffed inside of a deboned turkey and we're **sorry** we're forcing this metaphor. There is also the perhaps more apt "cherpumple" consisting of different pies baked into different kinds of cake and stacked on top of one another.

5

LOCAL GOVERNMENT

If the federal government is the big picture and the state the finer details, local government comprises the grainy pixels upon which the whole image is dependent. Though closest to you, local government can feel janky and obscure. This is the true minutia of American governance, and it calls to mind out-of-date computer systems, stale coffee, and the filling out of forms that might as well have been written by Harold Pinter for all their inanity. If we want to talk about the ground floor of politics and government, though, here it is. Stubby orange-brown 1970s carpeting and all.

You're most likely to have interacted with your local government after forgetting to feed the meter or trying to dispose of that old couch you've had since college. The parking ticket, the dump sticker—these are the purview of your granularly mighty local government. So, too, are your health, safety, and daily conveniences. Police officers, sanitation workers, firefighters, bus drivers, public hospital workers—most of our essential public services are provided by people employed at the city or town level. The power to govern is derived from state constitutions and then applied as each locality sees fit. "Locality" can mean any number of things, though, and every five years the Census Bureau attempts to define the multitudinous governing systems employed throughout the country. Here's what they landed on in 2017.

TYPES OF LOCAL GOVERNMENT
County

It's not just about the fairs, people, though the provision of deep-fried candy bars and enormous gourds remains essential to American well-being. Counties are established by state governments and break the United States up into a jigsaw puzzle of about three thousand pieces. Though all states have counties,

not all have a county *government*. County government generally takes care of parts of states not already governed by a city or town government, and this is more common in some states than others. Connecticut and Rhode Island, for example, play local governance closer to the chest.

The powers that be in a county government can levy local taxes (like personal income taxes, sales taxes); preside over county courts, correctional institutions, and roads and bridges; enforce regulations such as building codes; and appoint officials who aren't elected. Who those powers that be actually *be* depends on the system.

Commission System

This is the most typical when it comes to county government. Under this system, you've usually got a group of elected individuals, three to five people who together serve as the legislative and executive officials who run the county. They debate and vote on measures that affect the county. A sole commissioner used to be a more common occurrence, but at this stage in the American game, Georgia is the only state to have some counties with one person in charge. If the very idea of a sole commissioner strikes you as unfair, remember that these are elected positions. That, and a sole commissioner typically holds public forums to debate measures before making a decision that may affect a million-plus people.

Council-Administrator System

If you live in one of these systems, then you elect members of a council that serves for some previously decided term, not unlike a congressperson. These council members appoint (and can fire at will) an administrator whose job is to do their bidding—they come up with the policies; the administrator puts them into effect in the county.

Council-Elected Executive System

Similar to the council-administrator system, except in this case the voter gets to choose both the council members and the executive. The elected executive has more power than an administrator, too—they can veto policies, weigh in on decisions, and propose the county budget.

County Officials

Many of the people that run the show in this government system are elected by voters in that county. Whether these positions are elected or appointed by commissioners or council members will vary based on where you reside, and some of these gigs feel like (and, in fact, are) holdovers from a simpler, DIY era in American history. It may shock you to learn, for example, that someone without a medical degree or any relevant experience can be in charge of determining the cause of someone's *death,* but then we require zero credentials for the presidency in this fair nation, so. All of this is to say, if you've got a hankering to be county coroner, go ahead and throw your hat in the ring! Squeamish about dead bodies? Don't let that stop you.

States determine their needs and often lump multiple duties under the same role depending on the size and budget of a county. The council or commission makes calls about roads and bridges, public libraries, pools, parks, jails, and hospitals, and they need some backup to make sure everyone behaves and keeps things in order. You'll find most of these folks in residence at the county courthouse:

Coroner

This role started out in England as early as the fifteenth century and was carried over to America in the seventeenth. So, yeah. We can go ahead and call this one a holdover. The name comes from "corowner," a person who carries out the pleas of the crown. These days it means a person who determines the cause of death in cases where it is not obviously by natural causes. In some cases, the coroner is authorized to serve as county sheriff. In others, the sheriff, county district attorney, or Justice of the Peace is coroner by default. But what we want you to take away from this is, *none of those people need to have ever examined a body, living or dead, before.* A coroner is not, by the way, a medical examiner. A medical examiner must at least be a physician, if not a full-blown forensic pathologist. Some states use a medical examiner system instead, and the National Academy of Sciences recommends that *all* states transition into this model, which makes sense since the alternative is straight-up bonkers.

Treasurer

This is the money manager—they're in charge of collecting, disbursing, and investing county funds. They have to keep financial records and prepare reports for the commission, commissioner, or county council. They're also responsible for collecting certain taxes and going after you if you fail to cough up.

Assessor

The person who determines how much the stuff in a county is worth. They value the "real property," meaning both parcels of land and the structures on that land every few years and put together an "assessment roll" listing out all of the real property and its value in a given county. The point of all this is not to let you know how much your house is worth, but to determine what your property taxes are going to be. Throw an addition onto the ol' homestead? You're probably looking at higher taxes assuming the assessor doesn't somehow miss it. Fun(ish?) fact, property taxes are levied based on a budget system—commissions or counselors determine how much money will cover budgetary needs and the assessor has to make sure property taxes add up to that number.

Sheriff

Apart from enjoying the clout that comes with the title, this is the head law enforcement officer in a county. They preside over deputy sheriffs, who carry out the law. Sheriffs are often in charge of security at county courts, presiding over county jails, transporting prisoners, and investigating crimes. Most can arrest you, serve warrants, and issue tickets and citations. You also get a handgun, a cruiser that says "Sheriff," and an (often star-shaped) badge.

Prosecuting Attorney

The county's lawyer—they're in charge of prosecuting law violations within their counties that are not otherwise being prosecuted by a federal, district, or municipal attorney. Sometimes the county attorney takes on only misdemeanor offenses, other times they're in charge of going after violations of state laws. Usually, the county attorney also represents the county in civil suits and provides legal counsel to the government. This is one of the few jobs that tends to require you actually be a practicing lawyer in order to run for the office.

County Clerk

The institutional memory of a county, the keeper of the files, the filer of the certificates. This is the person in charge of vital records (that means birth, marriage, and death certificates) and often much, much more than that. A county clerk may be in charge of maintaining all court documents, administering oaths, maintaining the jury system, processing passport applications, filing physicians' licenses, issuing county IDs, filing property deeds, licensing notary publics, sometimes even officiating weddings. The maintenance and administration of records can be one of the most essential and high-volume jobs at the county level. Not for the faint of heart or the fearful of paper cuts.

Auditor

Look, nobody likes an audit. But we have them because they keep us in check. This is the job that makes sure nobody is cooking the books. A county auditor oversees all financial records in a county and is often in charge of administering the budget and advising the county council or commissioners on the state of a county's finances. The auditor is the financial accountability officer in a given county.

Municipality

Though you most certainly live in a county if you reside in these fair states, you may be under an even more diminutive government thumb. This is your city, town, village, or borough (the latter being reserved for only six states in the Union) government, which is granted the power to watch over us all by individual state designation. County and municipal governments often work hand-in-hand, with the city or town able to meet needs on a more granular level. Municipal governments are in charge of garbage collection, maintenance of city facilities, making sure we have clean water to drink, safe reliable public transportation, and police and fire departments. Not unlike counties, municipalities rely on certain tax revenue and fees for things like garbage collection in order to keep the plates spinning—sometimes that's a little saucer of a population (Jerome, Arizona, at around 444 souls), and sometimes it's a platter of a place (take New York, New York, at a cool 8.4 million folk).

If you're living under municipal rule, you're probably under one of two systems. There's the **mayor-council** system, in which you, the voter, elect both a mayor and members of a city council and the mayor's either legislatively strong *or* really more of

a ceremonial hand-out-keys-to-the-city kinda gig. The other, a **council-manager** system, is designed to leave the city council to its political aims while a city manager makes sure the city is, well, managed. In this kind of a municipality, voters elect either a council and a mayor, or the council appoints a mayor from within their own ranks. After that's settled, the council, presided over by the mayor, will hire the city manager to administer the policies they vote on.

The departments within a city vary wildly depending on location and population, but the city, town, village, and borough administrators are hired hands as opposed to the elected officials that keep a county counting. Get yourself a good job working for the city—you may not make much moolah, but you'll be rich in public servitude. And job security. You can pretty much just keep that gig forever.

City Manager

This isn't entry-level work—city manager is basically the chief executive officer of the dinky town or honkin' city. They're in charge of carrying out the city council's wishes and supervising alllllll of the other administrators. Non-existent in a mayor-council system, where the mayor's got real teeth.

Assistant City Manager

Reports to the city manager, and sometimes goes by the ever so slightly cooler "deputy" city manager. If a city has too many departments to manage, the assistant role pops into being to help the manager manage. Essentially a supervisor, it helps for an assistant city manager to be something of a people person.

City Attorney

The legal advisor for a city, town, village, borough—this lawyer will tackle whatever legal conundrum a municipality manages to land itself in. Depending on the size of the municipality, this job might be contracted out to a firm that deals in local government.

Finance Director

Think treasurer but smaller—this is the money manager for a municipality. It's all budgeting, accounting, and disappointing people by telling them what they can't buy.

City Planner

Also known as the planning director, this is basically playing Sim City but it's your job and you have to be a lot more careful and you're looking many years into the future. The planner works with city council to figure out zoning ordinances and determine what can and should and will be built where and when.

Public Works Director

This is the person in charge of making your life more convenient than it would be if you were living off the grid deep in the redwood forest. Water, sewage, garbage collection, and clean and relatively navigable streets all fall under the purview of public works.

Public Information Officer

The public information officer is basically the press secretary of a municipality, in charge of preparing press releases, making statements to the public, and coordinating interviews and media requests.

Police Chief

The chief of police may be in charge of thousands of officers (notably, in New York City, that number is a whopping *36,000*) and is the main responder to scrutiny of all kinds. Every major crime or tragedy awaits a statement from a municipality's police chief. Working for the government tends to mean dependable hours—this is an exception.

Fire Chief

The fire chief is in charge of people who put their lives on the line in the name of protecting the people of a municipality. They coordinate all efforts to respond to fire, natural disasters, and medical emergencies. Another one of those permanently on-call jobs.

Parks and Recreation Director

The Ron Swanson of municipal government. This is the person in charge of all of the parks and pools and skating rinks and basketball courts and recreational activities offered by your city or town. A robust parks and rec department elevates a municipality beyond providing the necessary services and acknowledges that sometimes we need a little beauty and an elevated heart rate.

Townships

This designation tends to be reserved for the quaintest among us. Relegated mostly to rural New England and the Midwest, you can on occasion find direct democracy alive, weird, and well in this dying breed of local government. The town meeting still reigns supreme in small pockets of this nation where citizens gather regularly to vote on taxes, policy decisions, and administrative roles within their town. You mean like in *Gilmore Girls*? We do. Places like that actually exist.

When a little more oversight is needed, a board or council will be elected to rule the roost. There's often a chief administrator or selectman of some kind. Functioning much like a mini county or municipal government, townships have roles like clerk, treasurer, and assessor. A road commissioner will make sure that there aren't too many charming country road potholes and a public assistance supervisor will administer financial and emergency help when needed. As populations have shifted, municipalities and counties have absorbed many townships across the country.

School Districts

Not all public schools are members of independent districts (some are run by whatever municipal government they exist within), but those that are are governed by school boards. These are bona fide independent governments that have the power to levy taxes, set a yearly budget, establish the educational vision for the district, and appoint a superintendent. They can even open and close schools. School board members comprise the largest pool of elected officials in this country and hold enormous sway over how education plays out in primary and secondary schools in their district. You know who doesn't hold enormous sway? The voting public who hires them. Only about 10 percent of eligible voters turn out for school board elections.

Special Districts

When we pushed our nation to its western brink in the mid-nineteenth century, very specific and pressing needs made themselves apparent. Water, for example. We needed lots of it because we decided to turn a desert into an agricultural hotbed. We are nothing if not obstinate, we Americans. It was around this time that new territories and states started to form special districts.

Usually these districts are tasked with one function. The El Toro Water District, for example, manages all water and sewer infrastructure in southern Orange County, California. Public Hospital District Number 1 in South King County, Washington, operates the Valley Medical Center. The Desplaines Valley MAD, or Mosquito Abatement District, does just what it sounds like in the western suburbs of Chicago. On occasion, a district will be multifunctioning or will be set up temporarily in order to repay a debt. Districts are run by boards or commissions, elected or appointed, and either tax district residents in order to pay for services or charge fees for services rendered (such as in a water, gas, or electricity district).

In order to qualify as a government in the United States, an entity has to possess some kind of civil office capacity—the public has to have directly or indirectly established the government. As far as districts go, this sometimes means that landowning members of a proposed district are the ones to appoint board members. Sometimes this means that, if a private entity established a district board, that board does not have the power to tax and the state has ultimate say in the fate of that district.

WHY LOCAL GOVERNMENT MATTERS

We're under no illusions here—for most, the very mention of the term "local government" makes eyelids heavy and stomachs grumble with boredom-induced hunger.

We know you skimmed this section.

Nevertheless, hear this: Local government matters the very most. Funding may originate with the federal and pass through state government, but it's at the local level that it actually gets applied. Schools, hospitals, libraries, roads, bridges, cemeteries, water systems, electrical systems, parks, public safety—the people who govern the things closest to you are, in actual fact, closest to you. The officials who determine the most of your life are not ensconced in state houses or the marble halls of Washington, D.C., but within walking distance, in ugly public buildings. Not only do you get to vote for most of the people who run the show, but you're also probably going to run into them at the grocery store. In fact, the person who runs things could very well *be you.*

A GOVERNMENT
BY THE PEOPLE

6

ELECTIONS AND HOW
THEY WORK

Walk into the voting booth, pencil in a bubble, poke at a robot, or punch some chads, and you've done your part to select the people who will make your laws and govern your life. No muss, no fuss. Here's your sticker, go home and wait to get really, really excited or really, really sad.

The nation's myriad voting systems and mechanisms are a source of perpetual confusion, fury, and mistakes. Methods vary from town to town, state to state. And then there's that "wait, what?" known as the electoral college—a last-minute addition to the Constitution that has tormented us ever since.

EENIE MEENIE MINEY MO...

VOTE HERE

TYPES OF ELECTIONS
General Election

In the U.S., elections for officials serving in the national government in Washington take place every even-numbered year, on the first Tuesday after the first Monday in November. Some states have their general elections at that same time, while others try to separate their elections from the federal ones. Some elections, like those to fill a vacated office, or for Native American tribal posts, may take place on a different schedule entirely. There are local and regional elections every year, and they are (sadly) often neglected in favor of the big flashy national ones. But the general is where you vote for open offices; president (if it's not a midterm), your state's representatives to Congress (all of the House and a third of the Senate), and whatever seats in your state's legislature are up for election.[1] This can be your governor, your lieutenant governor, your state senators, etc. But the name, general election, means that it's open to all registered voters, unlike most primaries or caucuses, which are open only to registered members of one party or another.

Presidential Election vs. Midterm

Like the old saying goes, "if it's an even year and there's not a presidential election, you're in a midterm, Gus." You're probably familiar with presidential elections. They're where we pick our commander in chief and they happen every four years and they're great and maybe why you're reading this book. But the

---

[1] *Every State Does It Differently* is the subtitle of the majority of this book, it seems. For example, in New Hampshire *every single position* is up every two years. Senate, House, Governor, you name it.

midterm! That beautiful, unsung lower-turnout affair! Midterm elections are radically different from presidential. First off, the president (almost) always ends up at the kitchen table with a hot water bottle on his head and a steak on his eye. Midterms are often called a "referendum on the president." With few (two) exceptions in recent history, the party that did really well in the presidential election loses seats in the midterm.[2]

Also, during a presidential campaign, candidates for the House and Senate usually align themselves with the candidate for president. But during the midterm is when you hear a lot of campaign messages like "I'm not a party politician" or "I disagree with the president on guns/abortion/marijuana/campaign finance reform." Midterms are an event where the waters can be tested for more radical party positions, as they don't have to be lockstep with the president. And finally, since so few people go out and vote during the midterms, your vote has *that much more power.* Seize it!

Primaries and Caucuses

These are the elections before the elections, how each party decides which nominees will be on the ballot.[3] Primaries are run by the state, caucuses are run by the party. We talk later about

---

[2] Those two times were Bill Clinton in 1998 and George W. Bush in 2002.

[3] And they are relatively new. Until the 1960s, party leaders chose their nominee.

the importance of knowing how elections work in your state before heading to the polls, but for primaries and caucuses this is *especially* important. Many states have a **closed primary**, which means you can only vote in it if you are a registered member of the party. Others have an **open primary**, where anyone can vote, though you can only vote in one party's primary. And others have a **nonpartisan blanket primary**,[4] where the two candidates who received the most votes proceed to the general election, regardless of their party affiliation. And Independents beware! In many states, voting in a primary automatically registers you as a member of that party going forward. So if you claim Independent, then choose to vote in the GOP primary, you have to reregister as an Independent. Many people do this on the way out of the voting station so they don't forget in a few years.

Caucuses are a bit more rare—only six states do them instead of primaries. They can take several hours, and they're held in gymnasiums and libraries all across the state. In a caucus, you and fellow voters from your district with the same party affiliation get together and vote (if you're a Republican) by paper ballot or (if you're a Democrat) by physically standing in a room to indicate your candidate preference until one candidate doesn't achieve a certain percentage of people standing in their corner and then those voters have to go stand somewhere else. Phew. They're fun and there are a lot of speeches, but book your babysitter early because it can be a looong night.

---

[4] That's one name for it. Traditional blanket primaries were struck down as unconstitutional in 2000, so there are lots of new terms for this system: "jungle primary," "qualifying primary," or "top two primary."

Two nominating events are worth noting because they are the *first*: the Iowa caucus and the New Hampshire primary. Candidates spend an inordinate amount of time in those states; you can find a photo of just about every person who ran for president in the last twenty years worrying down a corn dog at the Iowa State Fair. And while the candidates who win those contests don't always become the party's nominee, they have an enormous amount of influence in terms of fundraising and media attention. And legislators from those states have sworn that they will do whatever it takes to keep them first. Critics of Iowa and New Hampshire's earliness point out that they are the sixth- and fourth-whitest states respectively.

Some have suggested we do a national primary, where everyone votes on the same day. Or even a rotating primary, where four states are chosen out of a hat each year. But currently, there is no concerted effort to change this system. If it *were* to be changed, it'd be entirely up to the parties themselves to do it. It is discussed a little more each election, though. Especially after the difficulties in the 2020 Iowa caucus, when a shaky transition to an app resulted in a three-day delay before the full results were in.

Special Elections

A special election is held when there is a vacancy in Congress due to death, resignation, or removal from office. When it happens in the House, Article I, Section 2, Clause 4 says, "When vacancies happen in the Representation from any State, the Executive Authority thereof shall issue Writs of Election to fill such Vacancies." That means the governor of the state has to hold an election for the seat, and these can happen before or during the next general election. And in the Senate,[5] it's a similar process, **but** if a state's legislature has, in the past, allowed a governor to temporarily fill a Senate seat, they can do that in perpetuity.

All that aside, they're called special elections, but they're fairly common—there have been over 200 in the Senate and about 1,500 in the House.

---

[5] At least since the Seventeenth Amendment was passed, which abolished the system of State Legislatures appointing senators and left it up to a popular vote.

7

THE ELECTORAL COLLEGE

WHAT IS IT?

First off, it's not a place. There is no Electoral College campus, student union, or a cappella singing group. It's simply the way we choose the president of the United States. And one of the more difficult notions to swallow is that your vote in that booth in November is not for a president. Sure, it sort of is, but it technically isn't. Your vote is telling a group of electors who they should vote for in December. So how does this system work? Why do we have it? And finally, whom does this system benefit?

Preventing the Mischief

In "Federalist 68," Alexander Hamilton's essay on the benefits of an Electoral College system, he states that the people should have a say in whom we pick for president. But he also says that it's equally desirable to have that choice made by "men most capable of analyzing the qualities adapted to the station." In essence, sure, let the people vote for president. Go wild. But let's have some sort of educated, moral, manly bulwark between the people and the office. Why? Well, even though you had to be a white landowner to vote, the framers couldn't shake their fear of "mob-ocracy." Not all of them were well-educated, specifically in matters of national and international politics. These electors were to be men of high virtue, men who could see the high virtue and moral integrity in a candidate, and cast their vote for him regardless of how the proles voted.

Also, let's say a candidate who is entirely unfit for office promises everything to the American people. A candidate who has no understanding of how our government operates, who wins the hearts of the American people through deception and corruption. And the people are just not to be trusted! They won't be able to help themselves from voting for that candidate, no matter how they try. But a group of savvy, sage electors will certainly put a stop to that, won't they? Hamilton says that this system is an "effectual security against this mischief." Remember, the framers were, again and again, trying to prevent repeating the past, trying to build systems that preempt tyranny and absolute power every step of the way.

How Does It Work?

Each state gets a certain number of electoral votes (we'll get to the determination of just how many in a moment), and the candidate who wins a plurality[1] of the popular vote in a state gets all of

---

[1] Look, we wish we could say "majority" instead of plurality, because plurality is one of those words that just makes us Alt-Tab over to watch blooper videos from *Emmet Otter's Jug-Band Christmas,* but there's no other word that works. Because if

them.[2] If Candidate A gets one single vote more than Candidate B in California, they'll get all 55 electoral votes.

There are a total of 538 electoral votes, and the magic number is 270. Once you get that many, you can call it a night because you're the next president.

But there's many a slip twixt the cup and the first Monday after the second Wednesday in December! That's the day that your state's electors meet and actually cast their electoral votes. Each elector casts one vote for president, one for VP. And in late December, the House and the Senate meet in a joint session to tally up those electoral votes. The current VP, as president of the Senate, is in charge of the show.[3]

How Many Votes Does Each State Get?

The number of electoral votes your state gets is exactly the same number of representatives you have in Congress. In New Hampshire, there are two members of the House of Representatives and two senators. Add those up, you get four electoral votes. Pennsylvania has eighteen people in the House, so with their two senators they have a far more substantial twenty votes.

But this brings us to the larger question: How do we determine how many members of Congress a state has? This is a process called apportionment, and it's based on state population, so it all comes

---

there are three candidates on a ballot, the one who gets more votes than any other probably won't have a majority, they'll have something like 44 percent.

[2] We hear you, Maine and Nebraska. We see you holding up your finger and slowly rising from your seat, we'll get to you in a minute.

[3] On very rare occasions, Congress can dispute the electoral votes and launch an investigation into who was supposed to win.

down to the census. The more people in your state, the more Reps and therefore electoral votes. The House has been capped at 435 members and the Senate is 100, and since Washington, D.C., gets three electoral votes (and no representation), that's how we get to 538. And that number shall not (without a new law saying otherwise) change. However! Representatives and votes slide around every ten years as we get a new census. Fast-growing states like Florida and Texas are slated to gain a few seats in the House due to the 2020 census, and New York is going to lose some.

How Does This System Affect Campaigns?

Take a look at this.

This is a map of the total number of campaign visits Hillary Clinton and Donald Trump made to each state in 2016.

MAP REFERENCE:
NATIONALPOPULARVOTE.COM

California, Texas, and Illinois,[4] which provide a whopping 113 electoral votes, got one visit each! And New York got no love.[5] This is because there was no chance (in 2016 at least) that California, New York, or Illinois would elect a Republican, or Texas a Democrat. That hasn't always been the case, and it could change again soon, but currently there's just no reason for candidates to spend money and time there.

But what if we didn't have this system? What if we just had a popular vote to pick the president? Over 60 percent of Americans live in cities. New York City's metropolitan population alone (which includes counties in New Jersey and Connecticut) is 23 million people. This is *three times* the combined number of people who live in the ten smallest states! A switch to a popular vote would force candidates to spend all their money in those big cities. Different regions of the country, including many that already feel left out of current American cultural and economic influence, would be ignored.

Winner Take All

The system we use, where the winner in a state gets all the state's electoral votes, **isn't in the Constitution.** We don't have to do it this way. But just about every state does it. Maine and Nebraska are the outliers, they give two of their four votes to the winner

---

[4] It's worth mentioning that the single campaign event in Illinois was just across the river (and well within the range of media coverage) from Davenport, Iowa.

[5] New Hampshire and Iowa are subject to a tremendous amount of wooing not due to their electoral votes necessarily, but because their respective primary and caucuses are the first nominating processes in the country and, as they say in the Granite State, wicked influential.

of the state, but the candidate who wins in each of their two districts gets the other two. It's not uncommon for these states to have three votes for one candidate and one for the other.

A second hat tip to our northeastern chums, Maine is the only state (several cities do this, like NYC, but Maine's the only state) to have **ranked choice voting.**[6] This is where you choose your first, second, and third choices for a candidate. If a candidate gets more than 50 percent of the "first choice" votes, it's all done. But if no candidate does, the candidate with the fewest first choice votes is eliminated, and all the people who voted for *that* candidate as first have their *second* choice thrown into the tally. This continues until one candidate gets a majority.

But Maine and Nebraska aside, the other 530 votes use this "winner take all" system.

Your state's electors all vote for the same person. However, when the state's electors convene to vote in December, they *can* opt to vote for another candidate. This happens once or twice each election, and they are referred to as "faithless electors." So far, faithless electors have not had any significant effect on the outcome of a race. But things don't have to stay that way. If we continue to use a system that has a barrier between the people and the vote, what's to stop that barrier of electors from going rogue? And if you don't like the notion of having a person vote the opposite of how your state voted, *why even have that person there in the first place?*

---

[6] They did this in the 2018 midterm; it was decided by a statewide ballot measure in 2017. In 2020, it will be the first time ranked choice voting is used for a presidential election.

It's An Interesting System, But Who Benefits?

Ah, well, it depends on when you're asking. But one thing is for sure, the Electoral College has always benefited one party or one region, even at its very inception. When the framers conceived the Three-fifths Compromise, where enslaved Americans counted as three-fifths of a person for the aforesaid apportionment process, southern slaveholders saw this as a tremendous gift. Because their population, boosted by large numbers of enslaved, netted them many more electoral votes and seats in the House of Representatives, though the voting population (i.e., white males) was far smaller. It's no coincidence that five of our first seven presidents were southern slaveholders.

But who is benefiting from it today? This is some *very gentle tiptoeing* here, but according to a recent study out of the University of Texas, in a close race in the modern era, the Electoral College significantly favors the GOP.

One of the authors, Michael Garuso, said, "Today, Republicans are more likely to benefit from an inversion primarily because each state's representation in the Electoral College is equal to its number of U.S. senators plus its number of U.S. Representatives, meaning that each individual citizen vote corresponds to a greater share of the Electoral College for Wyoming than for a large state like California and Texas. Because, by and large, small population states lean Republican, this feature benefits Republican candidates."

There have so far been five instances[7] of a candidate winning the popular vote but losing the Electoral College. Each of these had different circumstances that led to that discrepancy, but they all had the same outcome. The person who got the most electoral votes became president.

Are We Stuck with It?

Abolishing the Electoral College would require a Constitutional amendment, which would need two-thirds of both Houses to vote for it and three-fourths of the states to ratify it. And it doesn't seem likely that those smaller population states would voluntarily give up their voting power anytime soon.

However, some state legislatures have adopted a workaround; laws that say their electors will vote for the candidate who wins the popular vote, and if a number of states with a combined 270 votes adopt that law, it is in essence a roundabout way of abolishing the Electoral College. Would Hamilton be upset? Possibly. But the idea that an elector is expected to be "faithful" might rankle him even more.

---

[7] In very recent years, 2016 (Trump/Clinton) and 2000 (Bush/Gore). Before that we have to go back to 1888 (Harrison/Cleveland), 1876 (Hayes/Tilden), and finally 1824 (Adams/Jackson).

8

POLITICAL PARTIES

I t's a part of your identity. It's like your scent, your religion, your favorite coat. When you're next in the voting booth you're likely going to be picking someone who has a little "D" or an "R" next to their name, and you're increasingly likely to pick someone *because* of that letter. Or because they're not the other letter. In a Pew Research Center survey from 2016, the majority of both Democrat and Republican voters said a primary reason they voted for a candidate was because the other party's policies were harmful to the country.

RED HATS AND BLUE WAVES

It wasn't always like this. Sure, colors have been used to discern sides on battle and sporting fields for millennia, but not in the American political arena. When color televisions were introduced into the majority of American homes, the big news networks started to use colors on the electoral map on election night. But these were arbitrary and inconsistent; one major network in 1992 even had Bill Clinton's victory states shaded red! It wasn't until 1996 that all three major networks agreed to the same colors: red for Republican, blue for Democrat. But what pushed us into the world of spectral division we inhabit today was an incident of national uncertainty. When either George W. Bush or Al Gore would become president depending on the result of a contentious Florida recount in 2000, America stared at a red-and-blue map for over a month. By the time the Supreme Court had ruled in Bush's favor, the die had been cast. Republican red states and Democratic blue states comprised our nation. These two colors took on the same visual weight as the elephant and the donkey, and it's quite possible they'll never change. That said, while the hues and animals might be around forever, what those words *mean,* **Democrat** and **Republican,** will most certainly evolve. Because that's how it's always worked. So let's talk about parties, shall we?

AMERICA, PARTY OF TWO?

It doesn't say anywhere in the Constitution that we have a two-party system. And the framers abhorred political parties in general. Party disagreements had led to so much bloodshed in England (which had weathered ten civil wars since 1088) and many of the colonists[1] came here to escape the most recent trio of them in the late 1600s. The word "party" wasn't used as often as "faction" at that time, and the fear of factions and civil war was

---

[1] Including George Washington's family!

one of the few things the framers agreed upon.[2] However, with the American system of elections, specifically the "winner take all" office of President, we are wedded to a two-party system.

WHY?

It might get an eye roll if you mention it at the Thanksgiving table, but the reason for this is due to something called Duverger's Law. This theory, basically, says that if you have a voting system where the person with the most votes gets the office, any office, you will always have two parties with a real chance of winning. Because let's say one party gets about 40 percent of the vote year after year, and another party gets 40 percent, and a third party consistently gets just under 20 percent of the vote; the office will change hands between the first two, but the third party will *never* get a seat. Add that to our now ingrained notion that a third

---

[2] The most scathing critique of factions (and admission that they're unavoidable) is in James Madison's essay "Federalist X," possibly the most famous of what we now call *The Federalist Papers*.

party by its very nature doesn't have a chance at winning,[3] and there you have it. Now there are some countries that have proportional representation, where multiple candidates on a ballot can be elected,[4] and in those countries you have many more parties with seats in government.

But not us! It's gonna be two to tango in perpetuity. Though that's not to say it's always been Democrats and Republicans running the show, or that the Democratic and Republican parties even stood for what they do now, not by a long shot.

HOW THIS WHOLE THING BEGAN

If we told you about a party that was pro-slavery, all about states' rights, a staunch defender of the natural freedoms of the (non-enslaved) individual, and wanted as *little government interference as humanly possible,* who does that sound like to you? If it sounds like we're being deliberately sneaky, you're onto our ruse, because those are the tenets of the original **Democratic Party.** Well, not necessarily the Democrats. Initially, they were called the "Republicans," but under the leadership of Thomas Jefferson, their devotion to individual rights immediately earned them the moniker **the Democratic-Republicans,** with the Democratic part being added by critics of Jefferson, claiming his notions were aligned with the cries of *Liberté, Fraternité, Egalité* from the recently revolting French. But this was the birth of what we now

---

[3] Also, third party supporters are going to feel pressure to cast their vote for a candidate who has a chance, leaving only a small contingent of die-hard voters devoted to their cause.

[4] Like New Zealand, Israel, Brazil, and the Netherlands, to name a few.

call the **Democratic Party,** the oldest surviving political party in the world, which bears *no* resemblance to the party of today.

The foil to the Democratic-Republicans was the big-government, pro-national-bank, "make the states as weak as you can" **Federalist Party,** with big wheels like John Adams and Alexander Hamilton heading the cause. Those two parties duked it out until the War of 1812, when the Federalists openly refused to support our armed rematch with England. Once we signed the Treaty of Ghent and both sides got most of what they wanted, the Federalist Party collapsed. There was a brief, rather groovy period after the war where the Democratic-Republicans had such a staggering majority of seats across all offices that we bordered on a one-party system. This was called the "Era of Good Feelings" and we've never seen anything like it since. It was so non-partisan that the 1820 presidential candidate, James Monroe, ran completely unopposed.[5]

But this halcyon era was not to last. When Andrew Jackson took the helm in 1828, he steered the Democratic-Republicans in a new direction. Jackson's party was known as the "party of the common man," and they won due to recent legislation to allow *all* white men to vote, not just property owners. They were all for power of the executive, against power of Congress, pro–southern business interests, and against abolishing slavery. Jackson was the one to remove the "republican" from the party name, calling it "The Democracy," and the **Democratic Party** was born.[6] And

---

[5] And won! There weren't a lot of exit polls that night.

[6] One opponent of Jackson called him a "jackass," and instead of attacking him with a cane, Jackson embraced the insult and even put donkeys on his campaign

what group rises to become our necessary second party? First it's a group called the **National Republicans** (no relationship to the modern-day Republican Party), who also called themselves the "Anti-Jacksonians" or "Adams Men." Those groups merge with Anti-Masonics and develop into the **Whigs**.[7] While the Democrats were the party of the people, the Whig Party was the party of *law.* They advocated for the power of Congress over the president, called themselves "conservative," encouraged higher education, and supported having a national bank. The Whigs and the Democrats went at it for a few elections, until an issue, *the* American issue, required resolution.

THE ELEPHANT IN THE ROOM

Yes, the Democrats were against abolition, but they didn't carry banners saying they were pro-slavery. Neither they nor the Whigs made it a part of their platforms, because slavery was so tied to geographic region that to legislate on one side or the other would guarantee a loss of votes. But with the U.S. expanding ever westward, the question of whether to allow it in these new states mandated taking a position. In 1854, a group of opponents to the Kansas-Nebraska Act, a law that potentially allowed new states to be "slave states," met in Ripon, Wisconsin, and started a brash new third party. They called themselves the **Republicans,** and the largest plank in their platform was to stop the

---

posters. However, it wasn't until 1870 that Thomas Nast used the donkey as a symbol for the Democratic Party, cementing it in our editorial cartoon vernacular.

[7] Notable trading cards in your Whig collection include Henry Clay, Horace Greeley, William Henry Harrison, and John Tyler (until he was expelled from the party for vetoing a bunch of Whig bills), and (initially) a young Abraham Lincoln.

expansion of slavery in America.[8] Other than that, their policies were aligned with the Whigs: national banks, higher education, and expanding the railroads. Their first presidential candidate, John C. Frémont, didn't win the 1856 election. But he did get 33 percent of the popular vote,[9] a strong enough foundation to set the scene for four years later, when a tall former Congressman from Illinois named Abraham Lincoln became our first Republican president.

And slavery, that issue that the Democrats and the Whigs didn't want to get into, was the cause of our (so far) greatest crisis, our bloody Civil War. Democrats in the South favored secession (with the solitary exception of future president Andrew Johnson, a senator from Tennessee), and Democrats in the North were split into "War Democrats" and "Peace Democrats." By the time Robert E. Lee surrendered in April of 1865, over 620,000 men had died. And less than a week later, Lincoln himself would die in a boarding house as a host of surgeons struggled to keep him alive after being shot in the temple by the Confederate sympathizer John Wilkes Booth. One of the attendees of the dying president noted that he was so tall they had to place him diagonally on the bed.

RECONSTRUCTION

Before Lincoln's assassination, the Thirteenth Amendment was passed by Congress, and in December of 1865 it was ratified.

---

[8] They did not call for its abolition, however.

[9] The anti-immigrant "Know Nothing" candidate Millard Fillmore secured 22 percent in this election, and Democrat James Buchannan won with 45 percent.

Slavery was abolished, and the Reconstruction Era began. The Fourteenth and Fifteenth Amendments came soon after, granting equal protection under the law for the formerly enslaved, and prohibiting denial of the right to vote based on race. And here is one of the most difficult and cruel chapters in Democratic Party history. Republicans had control of most of the state legislatures in the South after the war, and federal armed forces were stationed there to enforce the Reconstruction Amendments. This wasn't purely altruistic, it was in the Republican Party's best interests. Now that the three-fifths clause was no longer in effect and Black Americans were counted fully toward state population, southern states had a significant boost in Congressional power, and Republicans wanted to hold on to that.

However, the majority of Southern Democrats opposed any civil rights legislation. A coalition of "Redeemers" was determined to return the South to all-white, all-Democrat leadership. They achieved this, occasionally by peaceful political methods, but also through violence, voter suppression, and rigging elections. The late 1860s was also the height of the first iteration of the Ku Klux Klan, a terrorist group that murdered and brutalized Republicans, Black people, and southerners who supported Civil Rights. It took acts of Federal Congress to suppress the KKK, but after their dissolution other White Supremacist organizations like the White League out of Mississippi and the Red Shirts of Louisiana used similar tactics to get white Democrats in power.

The Republicans agreed to remove federal troops from the South in a bargain to secure the contested election of Rutherford

B. Hayes in 1876, and Reconstruction ended. By 1877, the Re-deemers had succeeded. Every single southern state was con-trolled by the Democratic Party.

THE SLOW AND TANGLED PATH TO REALIGNMENT

So how did we get here? How did the party that benefited from the KKK end up giving us our first African American president? It was a gradual shift; Democrats didn't wake up one morning, slap their foreheads, and say, "We've made a huge mistake. Let's become the party of Civil Rights." One significant shift was the New Deal. This was Democrat Franklin Delano Roosevelt's plan in the wake of the 1929 crash and subsequent Great Depression, and it dragged the Democratic Party toward a more progressive and liberal ideology. Meanwhile, the Republican Party, while its genesis came out of a desire to end slavery, focused now on more conservative northern business interests and less on Civil Rights. The 1932 election was the last one in which the Repub-lican Party got the majority of Black votes. Still, some Southern Democrats fought bitterly to maintain segregation, filibustering anti-lynching legislation in the 1930s and even running their own "Dixiecrat" candidate Strom Thurmond against the Demo-crat nominee Harry Truman.[10] But through the 1960s, '70s, and '80s we have this **Realignment.** Yes, the majority of Republicans supported the Civil Rights Act in 1964, but that same year they

---

[10] The Democrats still won this election, but by a very slim margin. This led to the famous "Dewey Defeats Truman" erroneous headline in the *Chicago Daily Tribune.*

nominated Barry Goldwater, a senator who patently did not. The Republicans began to get the support of the southern elite, and the Democrats formed coalitions with Black and Latinx voters. And in the 1980 election, Republican Ronald Reagan won every southern state with the exception of Georgia.

STUFF MY UNCLE SAYS

First off, let us say we feel bad for using this hypothetical uncle. Most uncles are lovely, but we need someone to simulate heated political conversation. But if your uncle, or your partner's parents, or (most likely) somebody on Twitter brings up the ugly histories of these parties, is that fair? Is it fair for the modern-day Republican Party to remind us they are the "party of Lincoln," and Democrats the "party of the KKK"? The answer is "we don't know and we'll try to keep our feelings to ourselves" on that one. Yes, the Democrats were pro-slavery. But they are no longer. Their current party platform includes planks about racial, gender, and financial equality. Yes, the Republican platform of 1860 was overwhelmingly anti-slavery, but it also

supported completely open immigration to the United States and full citizenship rights given to all immigrant citizens, which it often doesn't today. It is always good to investigate our past, specifically the uncomfortable role White Supremacy has played at every step along the way, but the only consistency of party ideology is that it has changed, many times, and most certainly will change again.

9

VOTING

HOW TO DO IT

Suffrage is a liberty hard-won and vital. When the nation first gasped to life out of that stuffy hall in Pennsylvania in 1787, very few of us actually had it. Enfranchisement was reserved, with few exceptions, for free white men aged twenty-one or older. The "right to vote," by the way, is not actually codified in the Constitution. You don't "have a right to vote." There are amendments prohibiting voting restrictions on the basis of certain categories, but there is *nowhere* in the Constitution or the Bill of Rights or the Amendments a line that says, "American citizens have the *right to vote*." So *who* gets to vote is in most ways still left up to the states. In the early days, that sometimes meant restrictions that included Protestantism and ownership of fifty acres of land or more. All told, between 10 percent and 20 percent of the population was allowed to cast a ballot when the Constitution was ratified.

This nonsense started to ease up over the course of the nineteenth century, and by 1860 almost all white male citizens over twenty-one were allowed to vote. In fact, in some states, you didn't even have to be a citizen. Meaningful voting parameters didn't make it into the Constitution until the Reconstruction Amendments following the Civil War. The Fifteenth Amendment granted all male citizenry the right to vote regardless of race or former enslavement. Of course, that bright and shining moment was quickly followed by oppressive state restrictions aimed at ensuring the disenfranchisement of men of color.[1]

---

[1] Life as a Black American in the Reconstruction South was a fraught one. Black Americans made up the majority of the population in Mississippi and South Carolina, were about equal to the white population in Louisiana, and accounted for

After decades of demands from ladies in white dresses, women won the right to vote in 1920. Just as with the passage of the Fifteenth Amendment, the Nineteenth was only as good as its enforcement. It would be decades of lawsuits, protests, and state efforts to disenfranchise before women, and especially women of color, would have any ease casting their vote. The Constitution continued to receive various shots in the arm over the years, granting enfranchisement to millions, regardless of race, sex, or economic status. Sure, it took a while, but pretty much all adult Americans can vote now.

Ostensibly.

As with all rights, privileges, and immunities granted to citizenry of the United States, the fact is not the practice. Voting is at the very heart of our status as a democratic nation, but sometimes you still have to fight for that right.

So this here is all you need to make sure that you get yours as an American citizen who's eighteen (or eighteen-ish). This is your manual to voting in the United States.

A word of caution, ye who enter here—the U.S. Constitution reserves the details of voting to the states.

---

just under half of the head count in the other Confederate states. This made Black Americans a powerful voting base—Ulysses S. Grant won the presidency in part because of this. Southern whites, now stripped of their legal right to own human beings, visited oppressive laws and violence on the Black community in order to subdue what would have been strong political power. Barriers such as poll taxes and literacy tests effectively disenfranchised Black Americans and poor whites, while violent intimidation tactics on the part of both the police and the Ku Klux Klan worked to keep whatever voters remained away from the polls.

CONSTITUTION 101: Article I, Section 4, Clause 1: "The times, places, and manner of holding elections for Senators and Representatives shall be prescribed in each state by the legislature thereof; but the Congress may at any time by law make or alter such regulations." You'd be quite right in noticing that the Constitution does not here specify the times, places, and manner of holding *presidential* elections. We find the Electoral College in the Twelfth Amendment and the provision for electors in Article 2. The presidential election process is de facto—we elect senators and reps this way, we'll elect Electoral College electors in the same time, place, and manner. As with almost everything in this book, we should probably lead with SEE: FEDERALISM.

Your pals in Chattanooga may have a very different experience registering to vote and casting their ballots than you do out in Phoenix. That is *fine*, provided you know the rules wherever it is you're playing. Election law changes from year to year and state to state, so keep your eye on it. Some new requirement may have cropped up, or some old barrier been broken down. The very best way to ensure you don't get the short shrift come Election Day is to do your research beforehand. We're going to make this system work for you, come hell or high water.

STEP ONE: Be a citizen who is eighteen. Ish.

You do NOT have to be a natural born citizen of these United States to obtain the right to vote. Whether you were born here or granted citizenship later in life, you are eligible to vote.[2] But you must be eighteen years of age.

Ish.

Why -ish? Some states have a rad provision that allows seventeen-year-olds to vote in primaries and/or register to vote if they'll be eighteen by the time of the general election. Some states allow pre-registration for *sixteen*-year-olds. Pre-registration means you'll have a pending status on your state's voter registration list, then be officially registered to vote when you turn eighteen. Your state or local election office will have the details.

STEP TWO: Meet your state's residency requirements.

You have to be a legal resident of the state in which you register. For many states, you also have to meet a durational residency requirement. In other words, you have to have put in a little time. If you just moved to Boise a week ago, you're not yet an Idahoan in the eyes of the state election commission. Depending on where you moved *from,* you may be eligible to vote in your old state if you won't meet the residency requirements of your new state by Election Day. Give the local election commission a call for that one.

Lest a state get drunk on its own residency requirement, the

---

[2] There *are* some exceptions to this rule—in many cities and towns, noncitizens are permitted to vote for certain offices like school board.

Supreme Court ruled in 1972 that thirty days should about do it to qualify someone for voter registration. In some states, the residency requirement is as short as ten days. For many, it was eliminated entirely.

STEP TWO AND A HALF: In many states, don't be incarcerated or ruled "mentally incompetent."

The former is more common than the latter, but both bear mention. In many states, you cannot vote if you are currently incarcerated, on parole, or paying fines related to a felony conviction. In others, convicted felons cannot register at all. Ever. The crime for which you have been convicted may make a difference as well.

As far as "mental incompetence" goes, certain states deny the right to vote to people who have been ruled mentally incapacitated by a court. If a court has decided you are not capable of handling affairs such as contracts, money management, or medical decisions, your state may also prevent you from casting a vote.

STEP THREE: Determine the deadline.

With any luck, you've been preregistered since you turned sixteen. But let's say your state doesn't allow for it, or let's say you were too busy hanging out at Rusty's with the Socs—if you want your name on the books for election day, you better make sure you register before the deadline.

What's the deadline? you ask. Depends on where you live. Would this even *be* America if every state didn't have its own thing going on?

See, your state may not give a flying monkey about how long you've lived there, but chances are they do have a registration deadline. This is the hitch that can catch you with your pants down, so *pay attention*. There are only five states (New Hampshire, Idaho, Wisconsin, Wyoming, and Minnesota) that allow you to register at your polling place on the day of. States come out with new voter guides every year, so call your state or local polling place to ask how soon before an election you need to be registered to vote. To be absolutely safe, though? Just make sure you're registered over thirty days before the general election.

STEP FOUR: Register.

First things first, determine whether you need to.

> *Have you never registered before?*
>
> *Have you just moved to a new state?*
>
> *Have you just moved* **within** *your state?*
>
> *Have you changed your name?*
>
> *Do you want to change your party affiliation?*

If you've answered yes to any of the above, time to get your name and details right on the books.

There are three ways you can make an honest voter out of yourself—by mail, in person, and online—but not every option is available to all states. Let's start with the one that is.

REGISTERING IN PERSON

By the way, congratulations. This is an exciting day. You might feel like wearing something special. Your favorite blue shirt. Your lucky loafers. Your grandpa's cardigan. Just something that says, "I'm about to become a viable voter in this state and I'll wear my 'I voted' sticker 'til it turns to faded mush on my sports jacket."

You can register at state or local voter registration or election offices, the Department of Motor Vehicles, military recruitment centers, and often at various state agencies that the state has deputized to register people.

BUT WAIT.

Don't you leave the house just yet. Most states require an ID number of some kind, from either your driver's license or your social security card. Don't have either? There's often a box for that on the voter registration application. You can still, usually, register to vote, but you may have to get an affidavit or something similar. Your state might require proof of residency when you show up to register—this could be the address on your driver's license or recent official mail—and *some* may require proof of citizenship.

REGISTERING BY MAIL

There is a National Mail Voter Registration Form. You can download this bad boy at the U.S. Election Assistance Commission's website, print it out, fill it out, and mail it in according to your state's instructions. Don't have access to the Internet? You can get this same form in person at any of the agencies where you register in person. You can then fill it out there and hand it over, or take it home and do it.

Not all states accept the NMVRF, and some may accept it only as a way to apply for something else. Because why not make everything just a little bit trickier? Keeps us on our toes!

REGISTERING ONLINE

If you were born after 1995, you have probably skimmed the above sections to get to this one.

Welcome! Thanks for buying this book instead of downloading it for free somewhere or just reading the Sparknotes. I mean, this book basically *is* Sparknotes. Also . . . *is Sparknotes still a thing?*

Anyway, not all states allow you to register online, but some do. To find out, call your state or local election office. Or, you know, Google it.

THIS TOUCH-SCREEN ISN'T WORKING.

STEP FIVE: Research.

No, this is not a necessary step to voting. But this is our book, and this is going in.

Before you arrive at the polls on Election Day, it behooves you to have a sense of who it is you're voting for. And not in the "my friends and family are voting for Candidate X, so I guess I will, too," sense.

Why? Why, why, why does this part matter? Why can't you just fill in the bubbles willy-nilly (as many people do)?

Well, you can.

But here is the warmest recommendation that you not proceed in that manner. Long before those pallies got together in Philly and figured out our current system of government, a little someone named *Thomas Jefferson* wrote a little something called the *Declaration of Independence* and included something that goes like this. Jefferson wrote, "Governments are instituted among Men, deriving their just Powers from the Consent of the Governed." In this government, you have the power of consent. Your *vote* is your consent. Your choice may not win, but your choice for *sure* will not win if you don't figure out who your choice is to begin with!

Many states require that sample ballots be made available to voters before the day of the election. These ballots will closely resemble the form you'll be dealing with on Election Day, and it's the best way to facilitate your research. Call up the election office, Google around for your state's voting resources, and obtain a ballot. Then spend, oh, five to ten minutes on each candidate. What's their platform, in a nutshell? What's their history? Find the candidate who best reflects what you want and need out of this nation, and you'll be able to vote actively. In many states, you'll have the opportunity to vote on referenda and initiatives as well. These can have an immediate and lasting impact on your day-to-day life but be worded in infuriatingly obscure language, so you'll want to familiarize yourself before you accidentally vote in favor of stripping your own rights somehow.

Some people may prefer not to get involved in what can often feel like a political circus. But whether or not you want to be involved in politics, politics *will* be involved in your life. It will impact you in significant ways, from determining the speed limits in your neighborhood to whether you have access to the healthcare that you need. Voting is the one chance you have to have a say, so go do it!

STEP SIX: Vote.

This is the hardest step.

It seems like after all you've gone through to ensure that you *can* vote, this part should be a breeze. Not so, gentle civic participant. Remember all that talk about rights and making sure they're enforced? 'Tis here that the rubber meets the road.

FIGURE OUT WHEN IT'S HAPPENING

We're going to bet that you miss more elections than you actually vote in.[3] There are so very many and most of them go by unnoticed.

Depending on what kind of election we're talking here (local, state, midterm, general, primary, special, etc.), it can sneak up on you. The general election happens every four years on the first Tuesday after the first Monday in November, so that one we know. Midterms happen halfway between a president's term, *also* on the first Tuesday after the first Monday in November.

And then you've got the wild cards. State and local elections are all over the place, happening at different dates and with varying frequency across the country. Most states have four-year terms for governor, for example, but some have two. And then there are state legislators, judges, school board members, sheriffs, coroners, mayors, and any number of other bizarro roles that we happen to vote for at various times.

The dates of primaries and caucuses are set by the states and announced when they darn well please or their constitution mandates.

You might be lucky enough to catch a sign at your kid's school reminding you of an upcoming election, but there's a reason voter turnout is so low for all elections but the Big Presidential Show. Most are just not widely publicized. If you're worried about missing out on these smaller elections, you can get your

---

[3] You wanna take and raise us on this one, we'd be *tickled*. Just keep in mind, we are not wealthy people, and what is "even money," anyway? Five bucks? Let's call it five bucks.

voting calendar shored up by calling the nearest election office or checking out your city and state websites. They'll be able to give you dates and times for all of the various elections.

And *by the way,* poll opening and closing times also vary from state to state, so make sure you double-check yours. See what we said about this being the hardest step?

DETERMINE YOUR DISTRICT

Who and what you're voting for will depend on where you live in your state, city, and town. This one is actually pretty easy—go to senate.gov and house.gov to figure out your representatives at the federal level, your state's website to determine your state senators and reps, and your city or town's website to figure out things like councilmembers, assemblymen, etc. All you'll need to know for this one is where you live.

FIND YOUR POLLING PLACE

You can call your trusty state or local election office to ask where your polling place is. Sometimes it's listed online! Sometimes. Often, the polling place will appear on the sample ballot that your jurisdiction should be mailing to you before the election.

Voting usually takes place in a school or community center, but you can't go to just any polling place in town. You'll be assigned to a polling station based on your address. If you show up at the wrong place, your name will *not* be on the roster and you *won't* be able to vote there. And by the way, the polling place can change from year to year. It can even be switched at the last minute for whatever reason. Think of your polling station as a moving target and be ready to move with it.

Many states have resources available for people who might find it difficult to get to the polls for whatever reason, so sniff around, call around, shout in the streets around. And if you're concerned about taking the time off work, well, you might have good reason to be concerned. Not all states mandate that an employer give you an hour so you can go do your civic duty. Even in those states that do, it may not be *paid* time off. Some companies have additional provisions of their own, and sometimes your boss is a regular Uncle Sam and their heart sings at the prospect of you taking a moment to hit the polls. Look into your state code, your company policy, and the patriotic eyes of your immediate superior for guidance.

THE ABSENTEE BALLOT

Now let's say you *really* can't get to the polls, because you're serving in the Navy in Bahrain or teaching pottery in Bulgaria or taking a personal interregnum in Bad Gastein. This is where the absentee ballot comes in. You may also decide to use this if you're in college out of state.

First step is to apply—you can usually download the application online. Some states will then mail you a ballot, others will let you download it right from the website. Fill it out and mail it in so it arrives by the deadline. Of course there's a deadline. There's always a deadline. For most states, it's Election Day.

Many states also have something called early voting. It is just what it sounds like. You can show up to an election office X number of days before an election and cast your vote.

If you feel your excuses for not voting slowly shedding like so many layers of winter clothing then our plan is working.

CASTING YOUR VOTE

You've registered, you've noted the day and time and place, you've arranged a moment off work and for the ride and now there you are standing in front of your local polling place and you're even a little nervous because we've made such a *thing* of this. Well, sorry. It is a thing. Here's what you can expect on Election Day.

Roll up to your designated polling place, and the first thing you'll see will be people with campaign signs. Whatever the weather, that part carries on until the bitter end. States have different laws about campaigning at polling places, and it usually has to do with how close to the building entrance you can be. Each state prohibits campaigning within the sacred space itself.

Depending on when you arrive at the polling place, you may have to wait in line. That's okay, you've brought a book with you! And it just so happens to be this book. Very flattering.

You'll check in and, in some cases, show a driver's license or some other form of photo ID. This varies by state, so make sure you check your state's voting requirements beforehand.[4]

---

[4] This one is big—if you know what it takes to vote, you'll know if you're being turned away from the polls for the right reason. Just because someone is working

Now, let's say you don't have an ID of any kind on hand. Or in your possession at all. Or let's say that for any number of reasons your name has been taken off the roster and you're quite certain you're in your assigned polling place. Almost every state in the nation has what's called a provisional ballot.

> **FEDERALISM 101:** The Help America Vote Act was passed in 2002 after the infamous hanging chad debacle in the 2000 Presidential Election. It was a sweeping voting reform bill and aimed to fix voting systems and voter access issues. It required that states provide information about voting, update their equipment, keep statewide voter registration databases, have voter identification and administrative complaint procedures, and provide provisional ballots—unless that state has same-day voter registration.

Even if you don't have the proof that you're eligible to vote, you can fill one of these out and an administrator will determine afterward whether your ballot is valid. Unless you live in one of the states that do not provide provisional ballots,[5] these are your magic words: "I request a provisional ballot and receipt as is required by law." The receipt part is what will allow you to follow up to be sure that your ballot was counted.

And speaking of the ballot—we'd love to tell you that it is a well-regulated, streamlined, consistent thing from state to state,

---

the polls does *not* mean they know what they're talking about. It's up to you to protect your right to vote. Go in there assuming the polling person could have the wrong information and be prepared to tell them exactly what laws and requirements you're meeting.

[5] Such as Idaho, Minnesota, and New Hampshire, which allow you to register to vote day-of at the polls, and North Dakota, where voter registration is not required.

but alas. States have all sorts of methods, so here's what you might encounter on the big day.[6]

IN-PERSON PAPER BALLOTS

The specific design of the paper ballot varies from state to state, but for the most part you'll feel like you're back in grade school taking a standardized test. You'll fill in the bubble next to your candidate of choice and then either feed that ballot into a scanner or hand it over to someone who will count it by hand.

DIRECT RECORDING ELECTRONIC MACHINES

A.k.a. a computer. Some are touchscreen, some involve buttons, still others use dials.

MAIL-IN PAPER BALLOTS

In certain states and for certain elections, you can *only* vote by mail. You'll receive your ballot well before Election Day, fill it out, and put it in two different envelopes for extra secrecy. You'll then sign an affidavit on the envelope itself and mail it on in.

BALLOT-MARKING DEVICES

For those with disabilities that would make it difficult or impossible to mark a ballot themselves, these machines come equipped

---

[6] What you won't encounter on Election Day are the butterfly ballot and the lever machine. After the 2000 election, where the butterfly, otherwise known as a punch card, threw the country into a frenzy of recounts and examinations of "hanging" and "pregnant" chads, the ballot was phased out entirely. The same goes for those iconic lever machines, which were falling into disrepair across the country when the Help America Vote Act gave them the final boot in requiring updated equipment across the country.

with Braille keypads and sip-and-puff devices that allow voters to mark their ballots by other means.

STEP SEVEN: Receive your sticker, wear it with pride, guilt your friends and colleagues.

Self-explanatory.

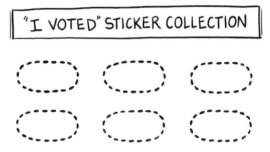

1776-The nation is revolting against Britain and voting in the provisional government was for property owners only, de facto limiting the vote to white men over the age of twenty-one (and the few unmarried property-owning women out there!).

1787-We scrap the Articles of Confederation and draw up our Constitution, which starts out by leaving voting standards to the states. For the most part, those states stick with the white male landowner thing. Two years later, a proportional handful of dudes elect George Washington president.

1828-First presidential election in which non-property-holding white men can vote in most states.

1848-A women's rights convention is held in Seneca Falls, New York. Frederick Douglass shows up and gives a speech in support of women's suffrage. The women present adopt a resolution that calls for voting rights for [white] women. So close, ladies, but maybe not *exactly* what Douglass was looking for? (Douglass would later have to defend the Fifteenth Amendment and Black men's suffrage against calls from Susan B. Anthony to give white women the vote before Black men.)

1856-North Carolina is the last state to remove the property rights stipulation—all white men in the United States can now vote.

1870-The Fifteenth Amendment is passed, making it unconstitutional to deny someone the right to vote based on race. Ostensibly, this means that men of color can vote. In reality, states began to institute poll taxes, literacy tests, and violence to prevent most and intimidate the rest of men of color who were eligible and attempted to vote.

1872-Susan B. Anthony tries to vote and is arrested in Rochester, New York. Sojourner Truth shows up at a polling place in Grand Rapids, Michigan, and asks for a ballot. She's told to hit the bricks.

1876-SCOTUS rules that Native Americans are not citizens and therefore cannot vote.

1882-The Chinese Exclusion Act prevents people with Chinese ancestry from becoming U.S. citizens—though a noncitizen who intended to *become* a citizen could vote in most places, this act prevented even the intention of citizenship, and therefore access to the polls.

1887-The Dawes Act gives Native Americans citizenship and therefore Native American men the right to vote *if* they renounce their tribal affiliations.

1890-Wyoming refuses to accept statehood unless Wyoming women can vote—they get statehood, women in Wyoming can vote.

1919-Native Americans who served in the military during World War I get U.S. citizenship and therefore the right to vote.

1920-The Nineteenth Amendment gives women the right to vote.

1922-SCOTUS adds people of Japanese descent to the list of people ineligible to become citizens of the U.S.

1923-Annnnd same goes for people of Asian Indian descent.

1924-Native Americans are granted citizenship across the board with the Indian Citizenship Act, but most states create laws that prevent them from voting.

1947-A Native American man sues New Mexico for not allowing him to vote. He wins, and New Mexico and Arizona are ordered to allow all Native Americans to vote.

1952-The McCarran-Walter Act says that all people of Asian ancestry can become citizens—Chinese, Japanese, and Indian people can now vote.

1961-The Twenty-Third Amendment gives people in Washington, D.C., the right to vote for president.

1964-The Twenty-Fourth Amendment says you cannot be denied the right to vote for not having paid your taxes.

1965-The Voting Rights Act is passed, forbidding discrimination in voting law and policy, and gives the federal government the power to enforce this act.

1971-The Twenty-Sixth Amendment gives eighteen-year-olds the right to vote.

1975-A change to the Voting Rights Act requires voting materials to be printed in other languages.

1993-The National Voter Registration Act makes voter registration available at Departments of Motor Vehicles and public assistance and disability agencies.

2002-The Help America Vote Act is passed after the hotly contested 2000 Presidential Election, mandating provisional ballots, updated voting equipment, state-provided voter information, disability access, registration databases, and identification and administrative complaint procedures.

2010-State lawmakers begin to introduce strict voter ID requirements, early voting cutbacks, and registration restrictions.

2019-Florida, Tennessee, Texas, Indiana, and Arizona enact voter restrictions, joining twenty other states across the nation who spent the decade doing the same. These include strict photo ID requirements for voting, laws that make it more difficult to register and stay registered, and restrictions that make absentee and early voting more difficult.

WHY WE DO IT THIS WAY

On October 24, 2016, Justin Timberlake posted a selfie to Instagram. The following day, the Internet was speculating wildly as to whether or not the man had broken the law.

For what crime, you may ask—being *too* good-looking? Hav-

ing eyes that are just too darn blue? Having a voice that is too much like an angel's?

It wasn't the *who* of the selfie, dear reader, but the *where*. Timberlake took the picture from a polling place in Memphis, Tennessee, with his ballot visible just behind that chiseled mug. He was there to cast an early vote for the 2016 election and the now-deleted selfie was intended to encourage voter turnout. It was certainly not intended to break the law. But break the law it probably *did*.

Tennessee is one of many states that prohibit the taking of photos or videos inside of a polling place.[7] Some states go so far as to explicitly prohibit the "ballot selfie." Considering the general aura of voting in America—protected, secret, susceptible to corruption—perhaps this strikes you as perfectly reasonable. We do *not* share our vote in America. For all the public pomp and noise of campaigning, the vote itself is a private act. It's a secret, them's the rules.

But them's haven't *always* been the rules.

In actual fact, for most of the history of voting in a place called America, there was no expectation that your vote be kept a secret. It would have been practically im-possible, given that voting was something done out loud, or at least in full view. From the early days of the colonies through the 1880s, it tended to be done *viva voce,* "with the living voice."

Some elections were held Iowa Caucus-style, with voters standing on one side of the room or the other to indicate their choice. Hands were raised, beans tossed into a hat. In many cases, your name would be called and you would ascend a platform to declare your choice for the gathered throngs.

The public vote was not just practical (you could vote

---

[7] Timberlake was totally fine, by the way. Well, duh.

regardless of literacy or the ability to write), it was considered the right and proper way to go about it. To vote in secret would have been lily-livered, opposed to the very principles upon which the new nation was founded. Democracy was not about private interest or personal preference, but about the republic. The union, the public good. Alexandria, Virginia, and Newport, Kentucky, actually *required* that voting be done *viva voce.*

The paper ballot always existed in America, but it was slow to spread. In those cities and states where it was used, a voter would write their selection on a scrap of paper and often submit their ballot in full view of others. A transparent ballot globe was more common than a box. As more and more people could vote, it did occur to some that a paper ballot was more practical than the chaos of *viva voce.* To address the issue of illiteracy, parties began preprinting ballots. You could cut yours out of the newspaper, or simply collect it from the party official who was handing it out at the polls.

Paper, by the way, did *not* mean secret. These ballots were very purposefully distinct—you could tell even from a distance whether a voter was voting for *you* based on the color and design of the ticket they handed over. It was a surefire way to verify that someone was voting as they pledged they would, which made for elections absolutely *lousy* with corruption.

Voters were paid (when not threatened) by party bosses the country over. A political cartoon by Thomas Nast shows William "Boss" Tweed, infamous New York Democrat thug, puffing a cigar as he glowers next to the ballot globe. True democracy brought to its knees by its own transparency.

You could quite literally buy the vote if you had enough green behind your campaign, and the corruption was common knowledge. For the vulnerable voter, Election Day often meant doing what someone more powerful wanted of you, lest your job or family be threatened. In his 1888 campaign for president, Benjamin Henry Harrison spoke to the decay of Election Day, extolling the virtues of the untainted ballot. Meanwhile, the Republican Party bought him the state of Indiana, and subsequently the presidency.

This was the last gasp of a public vote in the United States. We weren't the only country marred by election bribery and brawls. In Australia, the public ballot had led to an entire industry of criminal behavior around elections, and by the mid-nineteenth century, they'd successfully implemented a secret ballot the nation over. Massachusetts and Louisville, Kentucky, were already experimenting with the secret ballot the year that Harrison glided into the presidency. By the following general election, thirty-eight states were doing the same. It's around this time that voter registration started to become a thing in the states as a way to prevent someone from voting twice.

With the Progressive Era of the late nineteenth and early twentieth century came the cementing of a sterilized, private, protected voting system. Voting came to mean a single, state-produced ballot on which the names of all candidates would appear, to be filled out in a private booth and submitted without a single identifying mark. In most states, the secrecy of the ballot is a Constitutional guarantee. Voting is an intimate, personal, and somewhat stifled act. It has also become, in part due to legislative pushes to keep voters home, an act that just over half of us participate in.

For as long as we've been a democratic republic,[8] we've had systems in place to prevent huge swaths of that republic from having a say in how things go. The Constitution says quite a bit about voting, but nowhere does it expressly guarantee a right to it. The Fifteenth Amendment prohibits preventing someone from voting based on race, the Nineteenth prohibits it based on sex. But absent a central voting commission in this powerful democracy, disenfranchisement has always been a popular sport in the various states. After the passage of the Reconstruction amendments that ostensibly granted Black men access to the polls, Jim Crow laws throughout the South imposed restrictions like literacy tests and poll taxes that meant that poor and uneducated voters were de facto unable to vote. Women were banned from the polls in some states until 1920, but discriminatory laws effectively prevented most Black women from voting until the passage of the Civil Rights Act in 1965.

Even today, though the tactics are more subtle and more difficult to identify as explicit suppression, partisan organizations work to prevent undesirable voters from showing up to the polls.

---

[8] "We're a Republic, not a Democracy" is an oft-lobbed claim in the world of political science (or pseudo political science), but that is a false dichotomy. It isn't one or the other. It *is* true that we are not a pure direct democracy (for the most part, with the exception of certain state and local systems where a majority vote results in the passage of laws). We are, however, a representative democracy. And a constitutional democracy. And a republic, wherein citizens are empowered to vote for officers and representatives. If we're going to get as descriptive as possible, we could call it a Democratic Constitutional Republic.

During the 2008 Presidential Election, robocalls went out to households registered Democratic informing voters that they could avoid long lines by voting on November 5—the day *after* Election Day. Similar disinformation campaigns have involved telling voters that they could vote by phone (you cannot) or to mail their absentee ballots to the wrong address. Voter "caging" is a tactic employed by parties themselves, wherein you're mailed a certified letter, and if you're not there to pick it up, your name is struck from the voter roll under the assumption that you've moved or died. Some believe that election security laws effectively do the same thing that explicit voter suppression methods do. Voter ID laws, for example, make it more difficult for hundreds of thousands to get their hands on a ballot. The same goes for laws banning convicted felons from ever voting again in certain states—you won't find it anywhere in the language, of course, but this results in the disproportionate disenfranchisement of men of color.

The lesson in this era of orchestrated disinformation campaigns, voter suppression, apathy, and the like? You can make it better by getting the people you want into office. You know how you do that, eligible voter? You vote.

THE DOCUMENTS

When we were making episodes on the foundational documents, we spoke to a number of teachers. And one of them said that for all the activities, computer games, lesson plans, and videos, you eventually reach a point where you just have to read the darn things. And to a certain extent, it's true! But when you're six rereads into the Necessary and Proper Clause and your eyes are rolling into the back of your head, take heart. These can be hard. They can be hypocritical. They're being interpreted at this very second to support two completely contradictory arguments. There's no better resource than the source itself.

That said, if you'd like a little primer before delving into the vellum, here's a summary of the quartet that made us who we are: the Declaration, the Constitution, the Bill of Rights, and the Amendments.

10

THE DECLARATION OF INDEPENDENCE

IT'S NOT YOU, IT'S ME (BUT IT'S REALLY YOU)

It may seem a bit irreverent to refer to the Declaration (as many talented Social Studies teachers have) as the greatest breakup letter of all time,[1] but it truly has all the elements: Things aren't going well between us, here's why, I've tried to make this work, you haven't, and I'm leaving you.

Danielle Allen, who teaches the Declaration at Harvard University, told us it helps to think of it from back to front. The final section, which includes the language

---

[1] And longer breakup letters are out there; this one is only 1,337 words. Two pages, single-spaced—four if it's due tomorrow morning and you make it double-spaced with wide margins.

of the resolution Richard Henry Lee put before the Continental Congress, says, "We therefore . . . do, in the Name, and by Authority of the good People of these Colonies, solemnly publish and declare, That these United Colonies are, and of Right ought to be Free and Independent States." That is the action, that is what we're doing. The rest of the Declaration is an answer to that action. A justification for doing something . . . well, revolutionary—declaring themselves no longer loyal or obedient to their king. Thomas Jefferson, its main author, wrote to Lee in 1825 that its purpose was "to place before mankind the common sense of the subject, in terms so plain and firm as to command their assent, and to justify ourselves in the independent stand we are compelled to take."

But before we jump into the parts of the Declaration, let's have a look at how we got here.

A SUPER-CONDENSED VERSION OF 150 YEARS

British subjects in the colonies were technically under the rule of England. But Parliament was a 3,000-mile, three-month journey away! So the colonists were pretty much left to their own devices. There's even a term for this loose style of governing, "salutary neglect." The King appointed governors, but laws were created and enforced on a purely local level. Furthermore, England, a relatively small country with scant resources, benefited enormously from mercantilism, where the colonies sold them raw materials like cotton, sugar, tobacco, iron, and indigo, and bought processed goods back. This immense production and profit off of the land would not have been possible without the institution of slavery. By 1776, when more than 300,000 enslaved people had been sent to the colonies, there had been a growing movement in England to abolish it.

The system of salutary neglect starts to fall apart in the 1760s, when England accrues significant debt while fighting the Seven Years' War. The war ended in 1763, but to make sure France wouldn't be nosing in on the wealthy, unprotected colonies, England sent soldiers across the Atlantic to protect their borders. And now, since they were protecting the colonies, didn't it make sense that the colonies should share a little burden to pay for them? Prime Minister George Grenville passed a series of steep taxation acts on goods like paper, sugar, and tea. The colonists were furious about this, as they'd paid taxes on selling these raw goods to England in the first place—now they'd have to pay more when they bought the finished products back? And to make matters worse, the Quartering Act of 1765 mandated that the newly arrived British soldiers were to be housed and fed within colonial homes.

Unrest grew. Colonists boycotted British goods. England passed more taxes. In 1773, a group of men dressed up as Native Americans and dumped tea from a British ship into the Boston Harbor. England passed the Intolerable Acts in response,[2] tightening restrictions on the colonists, loosening them on British soldiers, and making Massachusetts residents pay for all that ruined tea. The First Continental Congress was formed in 1774 to figure out what to do about all of this; convince the king to go back to the merry old days of salutary neglect, or sever all ties and declare independence? They sent the Olive Branch Petition to the king, pledging loyalty to him but explaining the reasoning for their acts of rebellion, asking for a reprieve of all these acts. But before the petition even made it to King George's desk, the first battles of the Revolutionary War, Lexington and Concord,[3] had already happened. Then we get to June 7, 1776, when Richard Henry Lee first presents his resolution to Congress.

DECLARATION TIMELINE

If we want to celebrate our independence from England, we really should be doing it two days earlier. July 2, 1776, is the day that Lee's resolution was adopted by twelve of the thirteen

---

[2] The British didn't call them that, though. They referred to them as the "Coercive Acts."

[3] The "shot heard 'round the world," which refers to the shot that started the war, was initially used to reference the battle of Concord (in a poem by Ralph Waldo Emerson), even though the first shot was fired at Lexington earlier that day. Hey, and how about that? Nobody knows which side fired it!

colonies (New York abstained), and July 4 was the day the final draft of the Declaration itself was approved.[4] That night, the text was sent to John Dunlap, an Irish-born printer, who made roughly 200 copies. These look nothing like the elegant, handwritten copies we might be familiar with; these were typeset broadsides, meant to be dispatched among the colonies and read aloud. One of the Dunlap Broadsides got into the hands of British General William Howe, who then sent it to London to be read by King George III himself.

We wholly condone you celebrating American independence on July 2. Go have yourself a very small parade.

PARTS OF THE DECLARATION

There are four distinct pieces to it: A preamble, a statement of human rights, a long list of grievances, and finally the action. Here's our paraphrasing of those chunks.

1. Preamble

This part is not a justification for independence, but for the Declaration itself. It's a bit like a thesis statement; when a country declares itself independent, it's a good idea to say why. And that's what the following three sections are.

---

[4] Not signed!! It's debated among historians, but the consensus is that the Declaration wasn't signed until August 2, 1776. On paper, we're technically a Leo. Which makes *so* much sense.

2. Statement of Human Rights

Here we get a little lesson in government; we believe that people are given natural rights—life, liberty, and the pursuit of happiness.[5] And a government's job is to *secure* those rights. And let's say, hypothetically, a system of government fails to do that, it's the right of the people to "alter or abolish it."

3. The Airing of the Grievances

This is the long list of offenses. Twenty-seven reasons why we're ending this relationship. And most of them begin with the word "He," who is King George III. If you ever have a hankering to hear them in their entirety, NPR has a wonderful tradition of reading the whole Declaration aloud every Fourth of July.[6]

4. The Action

This is the final step. Because of the previous three sections, we have no choice but to separate.

---

[5] Some scholars claim that this trio has its roots in John Locke's *Two Treatises of Government,* in which he states the purpose of government is to protect "life, liberty, and estate." Others contend that it came from Sir Edward Coke, Sir William Blackstone, or even Dr. Samuel Johnson. Regardless of its origin, pursuit of happiness replaced "property" or "estate."

[6] In 2017, NPR not only read it aloud, they tweeted it. And some users, not recognizing it as our founding document, accused NPR of "inciting revolution." One user wrote, "this is why you're going to get defunded."

WHAT'S MISSING

There is a glaring omission in the Declaration, and it is slavery. An earlier draft contained a grievance that criticized the king's support of the institution of slavery, but it was removed.[7] Jefferson wrote that this was necessary to garner support for

> ALL MEN ARE CREATED EQUAL.

independence from South and North Carolina. So the poetic, inspiring, flag-waving statement that "all men are created equal" was good writing, but flimsy when it came to practice.

Within months of its adoption, a Black soldier and poet named Lemuel Haynes wrote an essay titled *Liberty Further Extended: Or Free Thoughts on the Illegality of Slave-keeping*, becoming the first in what would become a long line of activists

---

[7] This book is not the place to get into Jefferson's views on race, slavery, and abolition, but it must be pointed out that he did not envision an inclusive America. Yes, he wrote this rebuke in an early draft and went on to pass antislavery measures in Virginia, but he himself enslaved over 600 people during the course of his life. And until his death on July 4, 1826, he argued for the "expatriation" of emancipated Black Americans to other countries, calling it "greatly preferable to the mixture of colour here."

questioning these self-evident truths. Frederick Douglass in 1852 delivered his famous speech, "What to the Slave is the Fourth of July?" in which he asked, "What have I, or those I represent, to do with your national independence? Are the great principles of political freedom and of natural justice, embodied in that Declaration of Independence, extended to us?" And finally, Abraham Lincoln in 1863 delivered the Gettysburg Address, where he connected the ultimate sacrifice of thousands of Union soldiers to those promises of universal liberty in the Declaration.

Professor Allen told us that the authors and editors of the Declaration represented myriad views on the issue of slavery. Besides Jefferson, you've got John Adams, a lifetime opponent to the institution; Ben Franklin, who once practiced slavery but went on to liberate his slaves and actively support abolition; and the dozens of pro-slavery representatives in the Congress who made edits before adoption. However, there is a marginalized group who had no support from the authors of the Declaration, and that is the Native American people.

One of the final charges against the king states, "He has excited domestic insurrections amongst us, and has endeavored to bring on the inhabitants of our frontiers, the merciless Indian savages, whose known rule of warfare, is undistinguished destruction of all ages, sexes, and conditions." This language, which reinforces perpetual hostility toward Native people, regardless of their loyalty to either side in the revolution, has harsh reverberations that have yet to be addressed today.

TIME TO MAKE A GOVERNMENT!

Well, the much-celebrated committee of five has written their mission statement. Now it's time for the far less sexy committee of thirteen to get cracking on the rulebook. And it takes years of patches, nerfs, and buffs and a "firm league of friendship" before we finally get to We the People.

11

THE CONSTITUTION

THIS WHOLE IDEA SOUNDS PRETTY HALF-BAKED

The Articles of Confederation were something of America's post-breakup bad haircut plus weird tattoo plus sudden move to a city where we didn't know anyone. It seemed like, and maybe even *was,* a good idea at the time. But looking in the mirror a little while later, we had to admit that this wasn't *us,* and it certainly was not sustainable.

We'd waged a bloody revolution and then managed to cook up a plan that was mostly about getting the heck *out.* Out of Great Britain, out of paternalistic government. Just after drafting the Declaration of Independence, the Second Continental Congress appointed a committee of thirteen men to draft a constitution for this *thing.* A nation, sure, a brand-new independent nation, but what kind? What would it look like, how would it operate?

They had a draft of the Articles of Confederation ready for ratification by November 1777, but it wasn't finally approved by all parties until 1781.[1] As you might imagine, the former colonists were very much burned by their experience under a motherland that had gone from beloved if helicopter-y to cool, distant, and even oppressive. The new system would go light on central government with an emphasis on state sovereignty. And that most nefarious of motherland tools, *taxation,* would be replaced with the power to simply request money from the states rather than demand it by law.

If you're reading this and thinking, that is *not* how our government works today, well, you are correct. The first iteration didn't include a lot of foresight.

What could possibly go wrong?

What went wrong is war brings debt and the states refused to hand over the Benjamins. Oh yeah, and that's another thing. We didn't have any Benjamins. While the Articles granted the federal government the power to regulate currency, they didn't say anything about creating a singular form of currency. Nor did the Articles deal with trade regulation beyond letting the states do their own thing. This meant economic chaos, since trade policies varied from state to state. The federal government could declare and wage war, but they had to depend on the states to provide their militias. What if a state didn't *want* to provide a militia? Well, that's how you go from the United States of America to knocking at Great Britain's door again, begging to be let back into the fold.

Now, you're probably thinking, okay, no big thing, just amend

---

[1] Maryland the Unbending refused to ratify the Articles until they were satisfied that other states wouldn't try to lay claim to lands west of the Ohio River.

the Articles! Great thinking. Only problem is that the Articles were *really* hard to amend. A unanimous state vote was required to change the Articles, making the chances of successful amendment highly unlikely.

That's right, the Articles of Confederation were *so deeply flawed* that they couldn't even fix themselves.

Half-baked, indeed.

WE DON'T NEED ANOTHER HERO, BUT WE DO NEED ANOTHER CONSTITUTION

The fallout of this slipshod document promised to be deeply divided states and scattered rebellion at best, total financial ruin and dissolution of the wild-eyed democratic experiment at worst. If there was any doubt of this impending trouble, a six-month armed uprising of four thousand protestors in Massachusetts sufficiently shocked the framers into taking a second look at the system.[2]

The framers agreed, after much hand-wringing, hemming,

---

[2] Shays' Rebellion, lead by Daniel Shays, was in protest of the debt crisis that was resulting in the imprisonment of Massachusetts farmers and the seizure of their lands. After months of assaults on courthouses, the rebellion culminated in an attempted raid of the Springfield, Massachusetts, arsenal. After a violent confrontation with an army privately raised by the Massachusetts governor at the time, the rebellion was stifled, but smaller rebellions and pockets of resistance continued throughout New England.

hawing, and pretty things said,[3] to meet in Philadelphia and discuss how to amend the Articles of Confederation to suit the needs of the thirteen colonies, the mounting debt, the promise of westward expansion, and the pressure from other nations, friend and foe. A guiding principle for this convention can be found in Washington's letter to Madison on November 5, 1786: "If there exists not a power to check them, what security has a man of life, liberty, or property?" In other words, civil liberties are all well and good, but without a strong government to preserve them, they will crumble.

When delegates met at the Philadelphia State House in May of 1787, the intention was to revise the Articles. Believing his desire to heal the nation, coupled with widespread popularity and respect, would be integral to the success of the proceedings, James Madison secured George Washington as an attendee, and the convention promptly made him president. Of the convention. The other presidency came later.[4]

---

[3] One of the very prettiest and most telling is in a letter from George Washington to James Madison on November 5, 1786. "How melancholy is the reflection, that in so short a space, we should have made such large strides towards fulfilling the prediction of our transatlantic foe! 'Leave them to themselves, and their government will soon dissolve.'" In other words, we break up with Britain and no sooner do we strike out on our own than we prove to be a flailing mess. Think of the sheer delight the Brits would get out of our knocking on their door, tail between our legs. We need to do something to fix this, and soon.

[4] Washington knew it was coming, too, by the way. Which was in part why he did not want to attend the convention or meddle in the affairs of the youngblood politickers of the day. Washington was deeply concerned about the country he'd seen so many die to protect. But he was also tired. Sure, he was only fifty-five, but fifty-five was a little different back in the day. Never mind the fact that he'd won us a *war* while his estate fell into disrepair and debt, and now all he wanted to do was fix things up, make whiskey at Mt. Vernon, and read in his study. And he knew,

Washington sat at a desk on an elevated platform while everyone else debated things for *four months* over the course of a sweltering summer. Guess what did not happen at the 1787 convention? Some snappy revisions to the existing Articles. And guess what *did* happen? The composition of a completely new constitution. They wrote the framework for a new government, and that very constitution is still in effect to this day.

THE MUTABLE IMMUTABLE DOCUMENT

The U.S. Constitution is the supreme law of the land. It looms above Congress, above the president, above We, the People. When people are sworn into office in this fair nation, they vow to protect the Constitution. This document is both all-powerful and deeply vulnerable. We fight and die to preserve it, all the while wrestling with what it actually means.

The Constitution feels as though it came down from the mount, was chiseled onto tablets of stone, and yet it is a living document, changeable and dependent on interpretation. When we talk about what it means, often we are talking about how it's been used and viewed, historically. Interpretation of the Constitution is in the hands of the Supreme Court of the United States, so while we can give you the words, only those nine justices are permitted to determine the meaning.

Onward!

---

he just knew, that if he went along with things, these guys were going to appoint him leader of the nation. And damn it if he wasn't dead-on. Sorry, George. Your nation needed you.

WHAT IT SAYS

The United States Constitution is an intro, followed by a list of seven "articles" that lay out how the government will work. Each article is broken up into sections, and within those sections there are clauses, some with lofty-sounding names. There are some hard and fast rules in there but a lot of it is ambiguous. The order of this thing tells you what the priorities were for the framers.

It goes:

"We, the people."

Legislative Branch.

Executive Branch.

Judicial Branch.

The states.

How to change the Constitution.

All debts that preceded this Constitution are still valid and oh, also, this is the Supreme Law of the Land.

Here's what it takes to ratify this baby.

THE PREAMBLE

First, it says "hello." The Constitution begins with a preamble that is considerably more mellifluous than the rest of the document:

> *We the People of the United States, in Order to form a more perfect Union, establish Justice, insure domestic Tranquility, provide for the common defence, promote the general Welfare, and secure the Blessings of Liberty to ourselves and our Posterity, do ordain and establish this Constitution for the United States of America.*

What's the most important part of this government, then? We are. The People. It's the very first part of our most revered set of principles for a reason. Yes, the Constitution was in actual fact written by landed white male gentry. And *yes,* when the document was penned most of the population of the United States was either disenfranchised or enslaved. Over two hundred some-odd years of proliferated empowerment, though, more and more citizens have come to be included in that "We." The notion of the United States as a cooperative venture is in part what has preserved this democratic republic. "We" made the rules, and only "We" can change them. "We" get to decide who captains the ship, but it is and always has been *our* ship.

Then comes the light lift of establishing a just, peaceful, safe, thriving, self-determining nation that'll keep kicking 'til kingdom come.

1787

WE
THE PEOPLE
TODAY

ARTICLE I—THE LEGISLATIVE BRANCH

In a government of, by, and for the people, the lawmaking body comes first. Article I lays out the fact of Congress—two houses, alike-ish in dignity, a bicameral body—and how it's going to work.

You've got the House of Representatives, a reflection of the British House of Commons. It's large, members are elected every other year, and states get reps based on apportionment. Then there's the Senate—smaller, lower turnover (staggered six-year terms), and every state gets two.

Lest Congress forget its place in all of this (that is, under the thumb of "We"), Article One is sure to enumerate the powers the legislative body possesses. The first section of the first Article tells us that Congress has the powers "herein granted." Now, implied powers certainly become a thing later on, but this is still essential to the limitation of the people in charge. Congress's few though immense powers are enumerated, followed by a list of what states *cannot* do. This Article pretty handily takes care of many of the ills we suffered under the Articles of Confederation. It creates a limited, elected body that both represents the will of the people and keeps the people in order, and it reels in the wild-eyed, shoot-from-the-hip states.

ARTICLE II—THE EXECUTIVE BRANCH

We'd already had ten "presidents" before George Washington,[5] though the job was nothing like the position laid out in Article II. The single-year appointment presided over Congress and carried comparatively little power. In fact, you had more power as a delegate than you did as president of Congress. The head of the executive branch as described in Article II bears resemblance really in title alone to preceding presidents in the United States. But that title *is* important because of its simplicity and mundanity as compared to say, Elizabeth II, by the Grace of God of the United Kingdom of Great Britain and Northern Ireland and of Her other Realms and Territories Queen, Head of the

---

[5] And we're not counting presidents of the Continental Congress, even if it is a trick question on a Trivial Pursuit card. These were the ten heads of our nation under the Articles of Confederation.

Commonwealth and Defender of the Faith. It signifies that the president of the United States is one of the people, selected from the masses by the masses to preside over the nation.[6]

Article II tells us that the U.S. shall have a president, and that president shall be chief executive serving a four-year term. "Executive," in our case, means the person who manages the various agencies within the executive branch, implements policy, proposes a budget, and presides over a cabinet. We get the bare-bones qualifications for running for president here, the establishment of a vice presidency, and the election system by which the president and vice president will be chosen—the Electoral College, at it again. The fact of the president's salary is established, as is the succession should he be removed from office, die, or prove unable to do his job. The compulsory oath is in here, too, "I do solemnly swear (or affirm) that I will faithfully execute the Office of President of the United States, and will to the best of my Ability, preserve, protect, and defend the Constitution of the United States."

In addition to being CEO of the USA, the president is the commander in chief of the Army and Navy. This is where we start to stumble into some real powers. The president can pardon people, enter into treaties (with two-thirds Senate approval), and

---

[6] It's worth noting that the framers wrote the powers, limitations, and responsibilities of the chief executive with the soon-to-be Mr. President sitting right there. They knew that George Washington would end up being the first POTUS and he was literally watching them write his job description. Let's just say they weren't **not** thinking about ol' George as they worked out the ideal role for the leader of the nation, and their implicit trust in the man who sat on that elevated platform and gazed silently out at them might have had something to do with the constitutional shape of the presidency.

appoint judges and executive branch positions under the advisement of the Senate. He can also convene and *adjourn* Congress, though the latter has historically been avoided. Though this may seem like a pretty major power over Congress, Article II also establishes that the president ensure that law is faithfully executed in the United States, making him a steward of Congress's will.

The kicker of Article II is the Impeachment Clause—crucial in a nation wary of demagogy and devoted to maintenance of a democracy. Should the president commit treason, bribery, or "other high crimes and misdemeanors",[7] he will be removed from office if impeached and convicted. The House's impeachment and Senate's conviction powers have already been established in Article I.

ARTICLE III—THE JUDICIAL BRANCH

When we think of the judiciary in the United States, it's of a system proliferated across the country with district trial and appellate courts in every state in the nation. Those courts are presided over by judges appointed by the president and confirmed by the Senate. The Constitution only mandates, however, the establishment of one court: The Supreme Court of the United States. Lower courts are optional, though Congress has established ninety-four district courts, thirteen circuit courts of appeals, and

---

[7] This term, like so much of the Constitution, is a matter of interpretation. Constitutional scholars tend to agree that this means "misconduct," but that it needn't be *criminal* misconduct to be considered an impeachable offense, since officials should be held to a higher standard than the rest of us. Usually the deeds have to be considered intentional and/or an abuse of power that subverts the Constitution.

a handful of specialized courts. There are over eight hundred presidentially appointed federal judges across the country.

The first section of Article III says that SCOTUS justices "shall hold their office during good behavior," which has been interpreted to mean "no term limits." The "good behavior" thing has meant that justices can be impeached and removed from their seat, which has happened a number of times in court history. The justices are also guaranteed that their compensation cannot be lowered while they sit on the bench, meaning Congress or the president cannot retaliate financially if they don't like whatever decisions are being made.

The Judiciary is empowered to deal with cases having to do with federal law, treaties, multiple states or foreign powers, admiralty and maritime issues, ambassadors, and public officials. SCOTUS itself has original jurisdiction when it comes to the ambassador and public official cases, and suits in which a state is named as a party. For all other cases where the federal judiciary has jurisdiction, SCOTUS acts as an appellate (or secondary "appeals" court).

This article also solidifies trial by jury and defines treason—round these parts it means, and only means, levying war against the United States, joining with the enemies of the U.S., or providing said enemies aid and comfort.

ARTICLE IV—STATES AND CITIZENSHIP

The states and their reserved rights are at top of mind for the framers as they draft the Constitution. That's in part because the convention consists of the delegates from various states arguing for what they want and need out of the nation, and in part because this Constitution will be handed down to what are effectively disparate sovereignties which have, up to this point, enjoyed relative—if chaotic—free rein.

Article IV is a light touch. It establishes the doctrine of "full faith and credit"—states are required to recognize and honor the acts, records, and proceedings of other states. For example, our New Hampshire driver's licenses are not null and void in Nevada. States are also required to treat citizens from other states fairly, and not impose on them tighter restrictions than they would on their own citizens. Should a fugitive from one state flee to another, the receiving state is required to return the fugitive. This clause applied to fugitive enslaved people until the passage of the Thirteenth Amendment.

The framers granted the nation the capacity to expand with this article, providing for the admittance of new states into the Union. States could also be formed from exist-ing states, so long as the new state, the existing state, and Congress all agreed on it. Most prettily, Article IV guarantees a republican form of government in every state. In other words, Oregon couldn't join the nation as a monarchy.

SORRY, SASQUATCH

If you are a citizen of the United States, you can rest as-sured that whatever state you reside in will have a government that reflects the federal government. Finally, Article IV promises the states protection from invasion and domestic violence.

ARTICLE V—AMENDMENTS

Remember the big, glaring problem with the Articles of Confederation? I mean, okay, there were plenty of problems with the Articles, but chief among them was how nearly impossible it was to amend them. Not gonna make that mistake twice!

This article is short, sweet, and to the point. An amendment can be proposed if either two-thirds of the House and Senate or two-thirds of state legislators vote to do so. Once the amendment is floating around in the legislative ether, it can become a part of the Constitution only if three-fourths of state legislatures or amendment conventions in three-fourths of the states vote to make it so. This is called ratification.

That said, Article V also protects certain parts of the Constitution from this process. One is the slave trade. In short, it could not be limited by Constitutional amendment until after 1808—of course a moot point today, but a dark reminder of one of the Constitutional Convention's more insidious incentives. The other is state suffrage, and this one still has all its teeth. "No state, without its consent, shall be deprived of its equal suffrage in the Senate." Every state gets two senators unless it specifically consents to fewer than that and an amendment is passed to solidify that.

ARTICLE VI—DEBTS, SUPREME LAW, AND RELIGIOUS TESTING

It all comes down to money, honey. That's ultimately what landed the delegates of the several states in the stuffy chambers of the Philadelphia State House. The U.S. was in a lot of debt after the war, the government couldn't levy taxes to pay off that debt, and economic chaos was threatening to fan the flames of rebellion. So, guess what ends up in the dang Constitution? Essentially, all the debts we had before we wrote this Constitution are still valid. We still gotta pay them. This isn't somehow wiping the slate clean just because it's a brand new government, okay?

Secondary to the debt thing is the declaration that the document you are reading—the Constitution of the United States of America, any and all laws made in pursuit of the law of the Constitution, and all treaties—are the Supreme Law of the Land, and judges in all of the states are bound to abide by that.

The Constitution wraps up by codifying its own protection. All officers of the United States are bound by oath to uphold the Constitution, *but* (and the but is confusing, because what follows seems in no way relevant to the oath) those officers will never have to pass a religious test to qualify for office. Though it may seem irrelevant, this particular clause is cited by many as the framers' intent to separate church from state, a doctrine never explicitly outlined in the Constitution.

ARTICLE VII—RATIFICATION OF THE CONSTITUTION

This is the shortest article, and one that became mere dressing once its terms were met.

"The Ratification of the Conventions of nine States, shall be sufficient for the Establishment of this Constitution between the States so ratifying the Same."

Constitutional ratifying conventions were held in all thirteen states. In an effort to promote ratification in New York, three men from the convention (Alexander Hamilton, James Madison, and John Jay) penned a series of eighty-five essays discussing the merits and logical reasoning behind every facet of our new government. They wrote them under the pseudonym "Publius" and they were published serially in NYC newspapers. Seventy-seven of them were bound into a collection called *The Federalist,* and are now referred to as *The Federalist Papers.* It is unknown how influential these were in securing ratification in New York, but they remain one of the best resources for interpreting the Constitution.

Delaware was the first to ratify, on December 7, 1787. New Hampshire was the ninth, on June 21, 1788. And with that, we had it. Our Supreme Law.

But wait.

Notice anything missing here? Like maybe the single most significant set of rules that any American citizen will ever rely upon? You really thought we'd leave our civil liberties hanging?

12

THE BILL OF RIGHTS

Just for fun, take a second and ask yourself, "what do I really like about America?" And for a brief moment, push aside problems, injustice, cynicism, and even healthy skepticism. If there is indeed a glowing coal in there, what are the forces that fan it? There's a good chance that there's something to do with *freedom* of one kind or another. You can say what you want. The press can hold the government accountable. You can worship the god of your choice in the way you see fit. You can keep something secret in your desk drawer and nobody is allowed to open it unless they have a really good reason. Those freedoms aren't technically in the Constitution. They come from the first ten amendments to the Constitution, which were written by James Madison and are what we now call the Bill of Rights. And we came *this* close to not having it. But before we get into their creation or application, let's make sure we know what they are.

GET YOUR HANDS OUT

We adore mnemonic devices, and this is one demonstrated by countless Social Studies teachers across the country. Do it one time and you'll never forget amendments one through ten. Just hold up the respective number of fingers.

1. Take your index finger and point it to your lips, then to the sky, pretend to write with it, and then use it to make the "get over here" gesture. These represent the right to free speech, religion, the press, and assembly.

2. Two fingers, index and thumb, make a little gun! This is your right to bear arms.

3. Three's a crowd. You're quartering a soldier in your house and you have a right to kick him out.

4. Take your four fingers, make a fist, and knock on the door. It's the police! But never fear, you don't have to cheese it because they don't have a warrant and you have a protection against unlawful search and seizure.

5. Take your whole hand and cover your mouth. Then use it to pretend you're pressing the buzzer on *Jeopardy!* You have a right to not incriminate yourself in court, and are protected against *Double Jeopardy!*, being charged more than once for the same crime.

6. We're up to two hands now. Take the index finger of one hand and tap the wrist of the other hand, the "we're running out of time" gesture. You have a right to a speedy trial.

7. This is the trickiest one. Pretend the five fingers on one hand are a jury, and the two fingers on the other hand represent $20. If it's a civil case involving more than $20, you have a right to a trial in front of a jury.

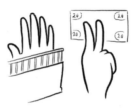

8. Not eight fingers, but look at the number eight on its side, ∞. That's a pair of handcuffs, and they're too darn tight! You have a protection against cruel and unusual punishment and excessive fines or bail.

9. Perhaps the most elegant physical depiction of a right unnamed: Put nine fingers in your pockets, keeping your thumb outside of them. Your pockets are the Constitution, and those nine fingers are protected by it. But your other finger, even though it's not in the Constitution, is

also protected! Just because a right isn't enumerated in the Constitution doesn't mean it's not protected in another way.

10. Finally, hold your hands in front of you and say, "Back off, buddy!" The encroaching entity is the federal government, and your hands are state government. All powers not granted by the Constitution to the federal government are the responsibility of the states.

Of course, each of these amendments has been interpreted to grant more than these basic protections, but now we're all on the same page.

DO WE EVEN NEED THIS THING?

There wasn't much debate or discussion about a Bill of Rights during the Constitutional Convention. Many states had their own bills of rights, and there wasn't really a fear that this new federal government would impede on individual liberties. However, it was brought up in the final days of the convention by two avowed anti-federalists,[1] George Mason and Elbridge Gerry. They argued that one was necessary, and it wouldn't be too much trouble to whip one up. Mason and Gerry volunteered to do it themselves, suggesting it shouldn't take more than an afternoon. The majority of delegates however saw this for what it was, an attempt to stall and scuttle the whole thing so a new convention could be called next year. Their proposal was shot down, and the Constitution went out for ratification without a bill of rights.

But its absence was a pea under the constitutional mattress, and some colonies couldn't let it go. Delaware, Pennsylvania, New Jersey, and Georgia all ratified rather quickly, but then things slowed down. Massachusetts, Virginia,[2] and New Hampshire said the Constitution should have one, while Madison and Hamilton[3] insisted it was not only unnecessary, but that adding it could be detrimental to the ratification process and then they'd just have to start from scratch. But the states persisted, and Madison vowed, against his own judgment, that if he was elected to Congress the very first thing he'd do was add a bill of rights. And he was, and he did.

---

[1] Neither of whom would go on to affix their name to the Constitution.

[2] Virginia was *crucial* for the ratification process, because it was assumed that the states which didn't ratify the Constitution would not operate under it. And it was assumed that George Washington would be our first president. No Virginia meant no Washington, and no Washington meant no Constitution.

[3] Hamilton argued in "Federalist 84" that we didn't need a bill of rights (and that its addition would be "dangerous") because the Constitution was *itself* a bill of rights that checked the powers of the government.

A "NAUSEOUS" PROJECT

At least that's what Madison called it. But you gotta hand it to him, he was elected to a majority-Federalist congress who didn't want a bill of rights, but he held to his campaign promise. One of the first things he did was ask each state to provide suggestions for rights to add to the Constitution,[4] and he winnowed it down from there.

His major opposition to the project was that if you enumerate all the rights of citizens, what happens if you forget one?[5] And also, where should they *go*? Madison initially wanted them to be put into the Constitution itself, but that was met with vehement opposition, as the words had been so carefully chosen. And it's Roger Sherman, that cobbler from Connecticut, member of the Committee of Five who wrote the Declaration, and creator of the Great Compromise, who proposed adding them as amendments.

So the giant list was culled and trimmed to a manageable twelve amendments, and they were submitted to Congress on September 25, 1789. The first two didn't make it through both chambers, so amendments three through twelve became our new one through ten.

---

[4] His first list had over two hundred.

[5] This was the rationale for the Ninth Amendment, which protects against just that.

> **NOT IN THE CONSTITUTION 101:** That's right! Our hallowed First Amendment, which is often cited as being so gosh darn important that the framers made it first, was actually our third. So what did Madison put as first and second? Number one was a specific formula to determine representation in the House. Were that amendment in effect today, the House would have about five thousand members. Number two was about Congress not being able to change their salaries between elections. This one actually made the cut, but not until 1992, when it became our Twenty-Seventh Amendment.

And there you have it.

Or do you?

You saw this coming, didn't you?

I mean, you've been with us this far, you must have suspected we couldn't end with a flag and a sparkler and a tear in our eye, right? That's right. So here comes the whaling metaphor.

Aedanus Burke, an opponent to the proposed Bill of Rights, once analogized it to "a tub thrown out to a whale." Fans of Melville will know of this practice, where to prevent the leviathan from striking your ship, you toss a huge wooden washtub into the sea in the hopes he will crush that instead. The main battle at the Constitutional Convention was how much power to give the states vs. the federal government. It wasn't about speech, or a free press, or owning guns, it was just about power. Sure, all the rights and protections in those amendments were endangered back in England, but nobody thought that was going to happen here.

And these rights, which hang on the walls of our *Civics 101* cubicles, seem as sacred and strong as iron. But are they? You can be the judge of that, but consider this all-important fact: They apply to federal law, but not state law. This means that the U.S. Congress cannot pass a law abridging your right to peacefully assemble, but your state sure can. America had no laws creating a national religion, but Massachusetts sure did.[6] The Supreme Court upheld this in *Barron v. Baltimore* in 1833, ruling that the Bill of Rights *only* restricts federal laws, not state. And this wasn't overturned until 1925, when the court ruled that they *do* apply to the states, but not immediately. It's called "selective incorporation"; these rights are, slowly, one at a time, incorporated into state law.[7]

Consider the First Amendment, which feels like it should be the bedrock of our national identity. The Supreme Court didn't rule that the First Amendment applied to state laws until 1925.[8] And it didn't strike down a law as unconstitutional under it until 1931!

JUDICIAL BRANCH 101: *Near v. Minnesota*: Jay Near, editor of the *Saturday Press* in Minneapolis, had accused local officials of being affiliated with gangsters. Minnesota banned him from printing any future publications, which the Supreme Court found a violation of the freedom of the press under the First Amendment. This was also the first case to deal with the concept of prior restraint, censorship before the act of speech even occurs. The court ruled that you can't stop someone from saying or writing something because you know it's going to be bad, you have to wait for them to do it.

---

[6] Until 1833!

[7] For example, the "excessive fines" portion of the Eighth Amendment wasn't incorporated until February 20, 2019. And the Seventh Amendment hasn't been incorporated at all.

[8] *Gitlow v. New York:* Gitlow, who was arrested for distributing pamphlets that encouraged the overthrow of the government, lost the case. But it got the First Amendment incorporated!

It took over a century of great movements, acts of protest, and sacrifice to hold our government accountable to the words in these documents. Like the Constitutional scholar Linda Monk told us, "ultimately, the Bill of Rights came from us, came from We the People, and it depends on We the People for its protection."

13

THE AMENDMENTS

TURN AND FACE THE STRANGE

We make mistakes. We forget things. The world changes and we have to change with it. That's why we have erasers, revised editions, tertiary mechanical failsafes. And that, my dears, is why we have amendments.

There are two ways to make a proposed amendment part of the Constitution, though our twenty-seven have only come about in one way; they start in Congress with a two-thirds vote proposal and go to the states for a three-fourths vote ratification.[1] This process is anything but straightforward. We made it

---

[1] The second way, a state amendments convention, also called an Article V convention, is more of a thought experiment than it is a concrete event. Because we have never actually had such a convention, there is question as to how it would be convened (the Constitution specifies only that states apply to Congress and Congress call the convention) and what its scope would, or could, be. And there's really only one way to find out . . .

easi*er* to amend the governing document when we wrote the Constitution. But we sure as anything didn't make it *easy.*

The first ten you already know—our Bill of Rights, that tub to the whale, proposed by Congress in 1789 after the Constitution made everyone totally freak out. The inclusion of these most revered of amendments was a slog—going from Madison's proposed nine to a full twenty after a House committee got their hands on them, then down to seventeen after much debate and editing. Then the Senate put the kibosh on another five, making it a final twelve that were submitted to the states.

By the time the list of proposed amendments actually headed out, each had been edited at *least* a couple dozen times. The Second Amendment—you know, the one that lets the little people possess deadly weapons—was edited over a thousand times. The drafting of Constitutional amendments *has* to be painstaking. For one thing, an amendment is a new *Supreme Law of the Land.*

It's a big freakin' deal. Our Constitution has proven strong and serviceable enough to last longer than any other.[2] Imagine passing an amendment that somehow compromised that integrity? So Congress takes its sweet time, because once it's done with these babies, the amendment is entirely out of their hands. State legislators take it from there. Which is how we ended up with ten, and not twelve, original amendments.

As for the other seventeen? Welcome to two hundred years of battle and debate.

THE ELEVENTH AMENDMENT

Proposed by Congress in 1794, ratified by twelve out of the fifteen states in 1795.

Federal courts are prohibited from hearing cases in which a state is sued by a citizen from another state or another country without the defendant state giving consent.

---

[2] That is, any other **singular** document guiding the operation of a nation's government and the basic rights of that nation's citizens. There are multi-text governments out there, like Great Britain, which has been doing its thing under a number of guiding lights since pretty much the thirteenth century. Still. A bunch of white, well-educated landed gentry (who couldn't have possibly predicted the staggering changes our nation has gone through) sit in a hot room for a few months and play Government Gods, and we're still operating by that playbook today? That's pretty remarkable.

This amendment was proposed after a 1793 Supreme Court case in which the court ruled in favor of a South Carolinian man who sued the state of Georgia for money and won. States balked at a decision that abolished a cherished principle of sovereign immunity, and Caleb Strong, a senator from Massachusetts, quickly drafted a Constitutional Amendment that would clear things up. This amendment ended up changing the line in Article III, Section 2, of the Constitution, which read, concerning areas of federal jurisdiction, cases "between a state and citizens of another state."

> **JUDICIAL BRANCH 101:** *Chisholm v. Georgia:* Alexander Chisholm was the executor of the estate of a Mr. Robert Farquhar. Farquhar had supplied the state of Georgia with goods during the Revolutionary War, and Chisholm set about suing Georgia to obtain payment for those goods. Georgia then refused to show up in court, arguing that they had sovereign immunity. In a four-one ruling (oh yeah, this is early-days-meet-in-a-basement-SCOTUS), SCOTUS determined that it had jurisdiction in the case of civilians suing a state and that Article III, Section 2, of the Constitution (on the jurisdiction of federal courts) nullified state sovereignty in the case of federal judicial reach.

THE TWELFTH AMENDMENT

Proposed by Congress 1803, ratified by thirteen out of the seventeen states in 1804.

Created a new method of electing the president and vice president.

The original Electoral College procedure in Article II, Section 1, gave each elector two votes, which they cast without specifying whether they were voting for president or vice president. Whoever won the most votes became president, whoever came in second became vice president. In cases where a candidate did not receive a majority of the votes, the House would select the president in a contingency election, and the Senate the vice president. This system worked so long as national darling George Washington was up for election, but showed its cracks as soon as ideologically opposed John Adams and Thomas Jefferson wound up president and vice president in 1796. The 1800 election was even worse, with electors attempting to follow a party ticket and ending up in a prolonged gridlock.

After years of debate and reformulating, Congress landed on a formula that would require each elector to cast one vote for president and one for vice president. The House-contingent Presidential Election is still a thing, but this amendment specifies that no more than three candidates be considered by the House and that each state get only one vote. The Senate holds the vice presidential–contingent election if necessary, but under the condition that a person deemed ineligible to serve as POTUS is similarly ineligible to serve as VP.

THE THIRTEENTH AMENDMENT

Proposed by Congress 1865, ratified by twenty-seven of the thirty-six states in 1865.

Abolished slavery and involuntary servitude except as punishment for a crime.

The first of the three Reconstruction Amendments that passed in the wake of the Civil War, this amendment contains the first explicit mention of slavery—an institution upon which the nation itself was built—in the Constitution. Though President Abraham Lincoln issued the Emancipation Proclamation in 1863, three years into the Civil War, this emancipation of enslaved individuals applied only to those eleven states that had seceded from the Union, and even then, only those that had not yet come under Union control. It essentially allowed for the continued bondage of enslaved people in select states so as not to alienate those states loyal to the Union.

Though no southern states were represented in Congress, the amendment did not pass the House during the first vote. Democrats argued against it not on moral grounds, but on the grounds of states' rights. After Lincoln won reelection in 1864, he made the amendment his priority. It took extensive lobbying on the part of the president and his supporters in Congress, but the House finally approved the amendment on January

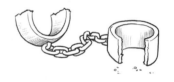

31, 1865. Though the Constitution says nothing about presidential involvement when it comes to amendments, the joint resolution was sent to Lincoln for a signature before it went out to the states.

The Thirteenth Amendment was ratified by eighteen states within the month. Lincoln would see Arkansas as the twenty-first to ratify before his assassination on April 14. Under the new president, Andrew Johnson, the southern legislatures were stacked with delegates deemed committed to reunification (if not the humanity of people of color) and, after assurances that the states would retain control over the rights of formerly enslaved individuals, the abolition of slavery was finally made Supreme Law on December 6, 1865.

THE FOURTEENTH AMENDMENT

Proposed by Congress in 1866, ratified by twenty-seven of thirty-seven states in 1868.[3]

All people born or naturalized in the U.S. are citizens and have equal civil and legal rights.

Congress passed the nation's first Civil Rights Act in 1866 (through the override of a presidential veto), guaranteeing citizenship regardless of race or former enslaved status, and equal civil and legal rights to all citizens. Fearing that this guarantee was ensured only so long as Republicans maintained a majority, multiple amendment proposals were drafted and finally the Fourteenth Amendment was transmitted to the states for ratification on June 16, 1866.

This amendment, which would make formerly enslaved people citizens with equal rights and protections, including the prohibition of state government from depriving them of life, liberty,

---

[3] Both New Jersey and Ohio had rescinded their ratifications at this point, so when Secretary of State William Seward certified that the amendment had become constitutional law, he did so under the condition that New Jersey's and Ohio's rescinded votes were invalid. Oregon also rescinded its ratification, but not until after the three-quarters ratification rule had been technically met. It wasn't until 2003, when New Jersey and Ohio re-ratified, that all existing Reconstruction era states officially, technically ratified the Fourteenth Amendment.

and property without due process, was refused by all formerly Confederate states with the exception of Tennessee. On March 2, 1867, Congress passed the Reconstruction Acts over Johnson's veto, putting these states under military control, requiring that they ratify the Fourteenth Amendment in order for their delegates to be sat in Congress, and requiring them to draft new state Constitutions. The amendment became Supreme Law under these compulsory provisions.

THE FIFTEENTH AMENDMENT

Proposed by Congress in 1869, ratified by twenty-eight of thirty-seven states in 1870.

A citizen's right to vote cannot be denied by the government based on that person's race, color, or prior enslavement or forced servitude.

Republicans in Congress had grown concerned that the new full citizenship of formerly enslaved individuals, making them full and not three-fifths of a person in terms of representation, would give southern states more power in Congress given the country's proportional representation. The enfranchisement of Black Americans was thought, therefore, to be politically expedient.

Fearing a Democrat-heavy Congress coming down the pike, the federal legislature quickly drafted and proposed an amendment that would codify voting rights regardless of race and formerly enslaved status. Though the prohibition of literacy tests and other methods of disenfranchisement were discussed and desired by some Republicans, ultimately Congress opted for the version of the amendment that was most likely to be ratified.

Most northern states, as well as those former Confederate states still under a military government, ratified quickly. Needing more ratifications, Congress passed a few more bills that would require Georgia, Virginia, Texas, and Mississippi to ratify if they wanted to be sat in Congress. A final, tenuous series of ratifications came in early 1870, granting Black American men the right to vote. Of course, this and the two other Reconstruction Amendments would be followed by decades of the Jim Crow South and the violent widespread subjugation and de facto disenfranchisement of Black Americans in the U.S.

THE SIXTEENTH AMENDMENT

Proposed by Congress in 1909, ratified by thirty-six of the forty-eight states in 1913.

The federal government can levy an income tax.

Prior to the Sixteenth Amendment, federal income tax had really only been implemented temporarily during the Civil War. It had been a wildly successful funds generator for the government, but was repealed in 1872. The government's primary form of fundraising was through tariffs—taxes on imported goods. Because working-class Americans spend a higher proportion of their income on goods, these tariffs affected them disproportionately, as opposed to wealthier Americans, and were viewed by many as an unfair burden that favored the wealthy.

The Wilson-Gorman Tariff Act of 1894 reduced tariffs slightly and introduced an income tax on incomes over $4,000, which would've affected around 1 percent of the population at that time. The Supreme Court shot the Act down on the grounds that it violated Article I, Section 2, of the Constitution, which required that direct taxes be collected based on a state's population.

Progressives continued to fight for an income tax, however, and after they attempted to attach one to a tariff bill in 1909, a handful of Conservatives thought they'd prove the idea worthless once and for all by proposing it as an amend-

ment to the Constitution. The idea being that because so many states were required to ratify the amendment, the ratification process would show Congress that an income tax would never make it in America. Much to their surprise, the states ratified, most in quick succession.

THE SEVENTEENTH AMENDMENT

Proposed by Congress in 1912, ratified by thirty-six of the forty-eight states in 1913.

Senators are directly elected by the people.

In its original iteration, the Constitution called for U.S. senators to be selected by state legislators. As partisanship deepened, states increasingly found themselves deadlocked over senate selection, resulting in seats that would sit empty, occasionally for years. Add to that the influence of special interest groups, and Progressives feared that the U.S. Senate was stacked with the wealthy puppets of a political machine that disregarded the will of the masses.

It was an era of reform, with more and more states opting for direct election primaries. Congress swelled in its numbers of Progressive delegates. As states contemplated a constitutional convention of their own to address Senate elections, Congress proposed the Sixteenth Amendment. Actually, they proposed *two,* one of which included what is now referred to as the "race rider," which would've in effect barred the federal government from interfering in the manner of holding elections, including those manners that discriminated against people based on race. An alternative amendment was proposed—one without the rider—and this is the one that passed Congress, and, eventually, ratification by the states.

THE EIGHTEENTH AMENDMENT

Proposed by Congress in 1917, ratified by thirty-six out of
the forty-eight states in 1919.

**Alcohol cannot be made, sold, or transported in the
United States.**

An amendment so infamous that the word "prohibition" became
inextricably linked to alcohol. Say the U.S. "during Prohibition,"
and nobody is going to wonder if you're talking about "of dancing."

By the time Congress introduced the Eighteenth Amendment, the Temperance Movement had, at times forcibly,[4] succeeded in state legislatures across the
country. Just over half of the forty-eight
states had anti-saloon and even prohibition legislation, and Temperance's ties to
the Women's Rights movement amplified
the effort considerably.

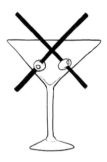

The Eighteenth Amendment was the
first to contain a deadline—if it was not
ratified within seven years of proposal,
it would be nullified. Of course, it was
ratified, and quickly by most states. Though the Eighteenth
did not ban the *consumption* of alcohol in the United States, it
made it difficult to obtain the stuff as it banned the manufacture,

---

[4] Temperance actually began way back in the eighteenth century in the states.
The Temperance movement birthed the Women's Christian Temperance Union
and the Anti-Saloon League as well as activists like Carrie Amelia Nation, a fierce
teetotaler who carried a hatchet and was known for violently attacking saloons,
breaking windows, smashing bars, and destroying bottles and barrels of alcohol, all
while singing hymns with the ladies who joined her cause. Carrie went to jail a lot
and paid her bail and fines with sales from her souvenir hatchets.

distribution, and sale of it, though it also didn't define what *types* of alcohol would be banned. Empowered by the amendment to enforce its intention, Congress passed the Volstead Act in 1919 in order to define the terms of Prohibition. Even some who supported Prohibition were surprised to learn that beer and wine, in addition to hard liquor, would be banned. Loopholes in the Act and violent gang takeover of the now criminal alcohol industry, however, made Prohibition really more of an idea than a reality.

THE NINETEENTH AMENDMENT

Proposed by Congress in 1919, ratified by thirty-six out of the forty-eight states in 1920.

Government cannot deny the right to vote on the basis of sex.

This amendment was first introduced in Congress in 1878. *1878!* And that was after decades of activism on the part of the women's suffrage movement. It was in 1848 that women and some sympathetic men met at Seneca Falls, New York, and drafted a Declaration of Sentiments that urged women to fight for enfranchisement

As new Western states joined the Union and included women's suffrage in their Constitutions, the women's suffrage movement gained attention and consideration in Congress. Though that 1878 proposal was shot down, it was followed by another that would've granted suffrage for

property-owning unmarried women or widows. You know, because a husband equals representation.

The women's suffrage movement was often at odds with itself, especially when it came to women of color versus white women,[5] and a unified effort was not easily established. Coupled with vehement opposition to the enfranchisement of women, especially in southern states, the Nineteenth Amendment faced many unsuccessful votes, and finally President Woodrow Wilson called a special session for Congress to roll out a proposal. Suffragists mobilized immediately, lobbying furiously in states across the country for ratification. It all culminated in a fraught lobbying process in Tennessee, where the amendment was ratified by a slim majority.

THE TWENTIETH AMENDMENT

Proposed by Congress in 1932, ratified by thirty-six of the forty-eight states in 1933.

The presidential and vice presidential terms will end and begin on January 20, and Congressional terms will end and begin on January 3.

The original text of the Constitution did not set a

---

[5] When the Fifteenth Amendment was passed, well-known suffragists like Elizabeth Cady Stanton and Susan B. Anthony spoke out against the enfranchisement of Black men before white women. Despite calls on the part of women of color, many white women in the suffrage movement refused to formally denounce white supremacy for fear it would alienate southern states and other members of the movement. Black women were excluded from conventions and marches, or told to march in the back. Suffragist Ida B. Wells famously defied these orders in the first suffragist march on Washington, D.C.

specific date for the beginning of terms for the president, vice president, and Congress. Congress, after the ratification of the Constitution, set March 4 as the start of proceedings and eventually passed a law requiring presidential electors be chosen in early November. This meant that there was a long "lame duck"[6] period between the election and the start of presidential and Congressional terms.

That lame duck period proved especially rough during the secession of southern states and the Great Depression, when the incoming presidents and Congress were delayed in being able to address these crises. This act basically limited that lame duck period and also provided a procedure for selecting a new president should the president-elect die before taking office.

THE TWENTY-FIRST AMENDMENT

Proposed by Congress in 1933, ratified by thirty-six of the forty-eight states in 1933.

Prohibition is repealed, but alcohol still cannot be imported into states that have laws prohibiting it.

Prohibition pretty much instantly spawned a black market and organized-crime boom in the United States. It proved largely unenforceable and public disillusionment was not far behind the passage of the Eighteenth Amendment.

---

[6] An outgoing politician whose successor has already been chosen. Because they're almost out of time in office, a lame duck is seen as lacking influence. However, because they're almost out of time in office, they can go a little crazy. This is often the period during which a president will issue pardons like they're going out of style, or push some politically inexpedient executive orders through.

The Twenty-First Amendment is the only one primarily designed to repeal an existing amendment. It's also the only one that was ratified by state-ratification conventions—remember that other option granted us by the Constitution—instead of the votes of state legislatures. The Temperance movement was dying down, but it still had teeth. To avoid state legislators bending to the pressure of teetotaling constituents, ratifying conventions populated by citizen delegates were opted for instead.

THE TWENTY-SECOND AMENDMENT

Proposed by Congress in 1947, ratified by thirty-six of the forty-eight states in 1951.

An individual is limited to two terms in the office of the presidency, and a successor to an unexpired presidential term that lasts longer than two years is limited to one additional term as president if elected.

Up until Franklin Delano Roosevelt's presidency, American presidents had limited themselves to a non-Constitutionally mandated two terms in office. *That* is how influential George Washington was. As our first president neared the end of his second term, he was exhausted and just *couldn't* deal with American politicking anymore. He said his goodbyes in a farewell

TWO RIDE LIMIT, MR. PRESIDENT.

address, and all subsequent presidents followed his precedent. Until FDR.

FDR was elected to a whopping four terms in the office of the presidency. The country was in bad shape, and FDR spent his twelve years and two some-odd months as president wrestling us back to health. And, you know, guiding us through the second World War. As soon as a new Republican-controlled Congress was seated, eighteen months after FDR's 1945 death in office, they took swift action and proposed Constitutional presidential term limits. It took nearly four years to achieve ratification, and several presidents have expressed their disdain for it since. Harry Truman, for example, called it "stupid." Cut 'em to the quick, Harry.

THE TWENTY-THIRD AMENDMENT

Proposed by Congress in 1960, ratified by thirty-eight of the fifty states in 1961.

Residents of Washington, D.C., can vote for the president.

Washington, D.C., is not a state. So residents of Washington, D.C., though they may be citizens of the United States, are not

citizens of a state. Given that electors in the Electoral College are apportioned to the *states,* this meant that D.C. didn't have a say in the election of the president and vice president.

Though the Twenty-Third Amendment granted U.S. citizens in D.C. electors in the Electoral College, it did not give the district the ability to vote for members of Congress *or* to participate in the Constitutional amendment process. When the Twenty-Third was ratified, D.C. was really and truly at the mercy of the requisite thirty-eight states—it had, and continues to have, no say in what the Constitution says about it.

THE TWENTY-FOURTH AMENDMENT

Proposed by Congress in 1962, ratified by thirty-eight of the fifty states in 1964.

The right to vote cannot be conditioned on the payment of a poll tax.

Following the enfranchisement of Black men in 1870, and then women in 1920, formerly Confederate southern states adopted a number of laws and policies that made it difficult, if not impossible, for minorities to vote in elections. The poll tax was one such tactic, which required the payment of a fixed fee before an individual could vote. This tax effectively disenfranchised a large number of the Black population in the South. So as not to disenfranchise poor *whites,* poll tax laws tended to include an exemption if a person's grandparent had voted.

The poll tax was the subject of legislative debate for

decades. FDR condemned the policy, but attempted legislation to eliminate it failed in the face of southern opposition. Because the Constitution was often cited by those politicians committed to their state's poll tax, opponents to the tax suggested a Constitutional amendment as the best course of action.

With limited southern support, the poll tax prohibition passed. Attempts to disenfranchise Black voters, however, remained in the form of, for example, Alabama's literacy test.[7]

THE TWENTY-FIFTH AMENDMENT

Proposed by Congress in 1965, ratified by thirty-eight of the fifty states in 1967.

The vice president becomes president, not *acting* president, if the president dies or is removed from office. Also establishes a procedure for filling the vice president seat and establishes what to do in the case of presidential disability.

The Constitution was (shocker) just a bit ambiguous on the subject of vice presidential succession. This amendment clarified that assuming the powers and duties of president of the United States made the vice president the new president, not just an acting president. This was done in order to ensure that a president who resigned could not just step back into office.

The vice presidency, in the case of its vacancy, had a bad historical habit of remaining unfilled in cases of the VP ascending

---

[7] Which included an oral portion in which respondents had to recite answers from memory. The registrar had discretion over what portions of the test they would administer (and therefore how difficult it would be).

to the presidency. This amendment ensures that the new president nominates a vice president to be approved by Congress so that the seat may be quickly filled.

Finally, the Twenty-Fifth takes care of the little problem of what to do when the president is, say, unconscious on an operating table and something big goes down in the country. Who is in charge? This amendment allows the president to declare, in writing, that he is temporarily transferring his duties to the vice president in anticipation of being indisposed. Another written statement is required to transfer the job back. In the event that the president is unable (or unwilling) to transfer these duties, the VP, together with members of the Cabinet or Congress, can effectively do the same thing.

Reagan invoked a temporary transfer of power during a surgery to remove a colonic lesion. George W. Bush did it *twice,* during his two colonoscopies while in office.

THE TWENTY-SIXTH AMENDMENT

Proposed by Congress in 1971, ratified by thirty-eight of the
fifty states in 1971.

**The government cannot deny citizens eighteen years
of age or older the right to vote.**

Though attempts to lower the voting age from twenty-one to
eighteen had cropped up in the past, they'd never gained enough
support to actually amend the Constitution. An amendment to
the 1965 Voting Rights Act attempted to lower the voting age to
eighteen in all local, state, and federal elections, but the Supreme
Court upheld only the federal provision, allowing states to maintain the age of twenty-one as the threshold for state and local
elections.

While opponents to the
lower voting age argued the im-
maturity of eighteen-year-olds, a
growing student activism movement coupled with the calls of
Vietnam War soldiers arguing
that if a citizen were old enough
to be conscripted into war (the
draft applied to young men aged

eighteen and older) then he was old enough to vote. The Twenty-
Sixth Amendment was ratified faster than any in U.S. history,
leaving Capitol Hill on March 23, 1971, and achieving ratification on July 1, 1971.

THE TWENTY-SEVENTH AMENDMENT

Proposed by Congress in 1789, ratified by thirty-eight of the
fifty states in 1992.

**A law pertaining to Congressional compensation
cannot take effect until the next Congressional term
begins.**

This is a fun one. Following the fastest ratification in American history was the slowest. Two hundred and two years, seven months, and ten days. So, what the heck happened?

Remember the Bill of Rights? Those ten glorious amendments that granted us civil liberties, way, way back in the day? Yeah, this was supposed to be one of them. In fact, this was the second of the twelve articles proposed to the states for ratification. But after states failed to ratify it, it was forgotten, lost to history.

Until Gregory Watson got a "C."

Watson was a sophomore at the University of Texas at Austin in 1982, writing a paper on governmental process for a political science class. He stumbled upon the existence of this yet unratified amendment and argued that, as the amendment did not contain a time limit, it could still be ratified. Watson received a "C" from the teaching assistant, then appealed his grade to the professor and was denied. The "C" stood, so Watson thumbed his nose and launched a nationwide campaign to get states to finally ratify the amendment.

> **JUDICIAL BRANCH 101:** In *Coleman v. Miller* in 1939, the Supreme Court ruled that if Congress does not include a deadline attached to a proposed amendment, then that amendment remains pending before state legislatures. It is then up to Congress to decide, if three-fourths of states do indeed ratify at some point, whether too much time has elapsed since the proposal of the amendment to validate state ratification.

Watson's campaign was a sweeping success, and the Twenty-Seventh Amendment was ratified on May 5, 1992. Twenty-five years later, at the urging of a professor in UT's government department, Watson's long-since-retired teacher, Sharon Waite, signed a grade change form amending Watson's "C" and making it an "A+." I mean. He did *change the Constitution* after all.

PENDING

There have been over ten thousand attempts to amend the United States Constitution, but very few make it over that Congressional threshold and into the hands of the people. Of those, seven (as of the writing of this book) haven't achieved ratification. Yet.

CONGRESSIONAL APPORTIONMENT AMENDMENT

Proposed by Congress in 1789.

This amendment sets up a formula, based on state population, for determining the number of seats in the House of Representatives. Had it been ratified and upheld, we'd have over 6,500 seats in the House instead of the slightly more manageable statute-limited 435. This amendment is still pending.

TITLES OF NOBILITY AMENDMENT
Proposed by Congress in 1810.

This one says that if an American citizen accepts a title of nobility from another nation without Congressional approval, they cease to be an American citizen. Try telling that to Meghan Markle. This amendment is still pending.

SLAVERY AMENDMENT
Proposed by Congress in 1861.

This amendment would have banned the federal government from abolishing slavery in states where it already existed. It is only *very technically* still pending.

CHILD LABOR AMENDMENT
Proposed by Congress in 1924.

This would have authorized Congress to regulate labor of people under the age of eighteen. The Fair Labor Standards Act of 1938 pretty much took care of that, but this amendment is still pending.

EQUAL RIGHTS AMENDMENT
Proposed by Congress in 1972.

This amendment would have Constitutionally cemented equal legal rights for all people in the United States regardless of sex. The idea was to bring an end to distinctions between men and women when it came to property, employment, divorce, parenting, etc. Congress had originally set a deadline of March 22, 1979, then extended it to June 30, 1982, but the amendment did not receive the requisite ratifications in the time allotted. Virginia did ratify the amendment in early 2020, but at the time of this printing the validity of that ratification is still being debated.

DISTRICT OF COLUMBIA VOTING RIGHTS AMENDMENT
Proposed by Congress in 1978.

This would have repealed the Twenty-Third Amendment and replaced it with the additional provision of Washington, D.C.'s ostensible state status in Congressional elections. A seven-year deadline is built into the language of this amendment, and it failed to ratify in the time allotted.

BALANCED BUDGET AMENDMENT
Proposed by Congress in 1991.

This would have required federal Government spending to not exceed net revenue unless in times of war or if two-thirds of Congress resolved that a national economic emergency permitted suspension in a given fiscal year. This also failed to ratify in the seven years allotted for state consideration.

THE ROBES

14

SUPREME COURT CASES
EVERYONE SHOULD KNOW

This chapter is a primer on the fifteen SCOTUS decisions that we feel every American should know. Reading opinions from the highest court in the land can be difficult, especially if they're from the nineteenth century. But in a system where bills in Congress often clock in at over a thousand pages, the reasonings given for a court decision are relatively brief. It's easy to forget that almost all the justices at one time were lawyers, people whose job was to make things as clear as possible for judges and juries, so take a crack at reading a few. As we said earlier, these opinions are "footnotes to the Constitution," and their interpretation of the supreme law of the land is what makes it a living document.

But before you tuck in, remember that the Supreme Court is not infallible and its rulings by no means permanent. Many of its own decisions[1] have been reversed, for good or for ill.

---

[1] Two hundred thirty-six times and counting.

MARBURY V. MADISON
—

Decided in 1803: Citing the powers granted to them under Article III, Section 2, of the Constitution, the Supreme Court declares the provisions of the 1789 Judiciary Act unconstitutional, therefore establishing judicial review.

The Case

This one is the scourge of many an AP U.S. History student. It's got a few byzantine twists and turns, but it's really more about the punch line than the joke. John Adams lost the 1800 election to Thomas Jefferson, but Jefferson wasn't to be sworn in until March 4, 1801.

> **EXECUTIVE BRANCH 101:** Adams was in a "lame duck" presidency here. The Twentieth Amendment moved this date up to January 3, significantly reducing this rather awkward transition. When Barack Obama gave his farewell speech in 2017 and the crowd refused to stop cheering, he said, "You can tell that I'm a lame duck because nobody's following instructions."

Instead of riding out his end of term quietly, Adams and his Federalist Congress passed the Judiciary Act of 1801 (based on the Judiciary Act of 1789), granting them the power to pack the federal courts with judges from their party in an effort to preserve their power in the judicial branch, even though they'd lost control of the Congress and the presidency. By the day of Jefferson's inauguration, they had appointed sixteen circuit court judges and forty-two Justices of the Peace. Not all of the judge commissions were delivered in time, however. Jefferson came into the office and saw a fat stack of them with a note saying "kindly deliver these to your political enemies."[2] One of those judges to be, William Marbury, never received his commission. And this guy *really* wanted to be a JP. Marbury petitioned the Supreme Court to order a "Writ of Mandamus" to the new secretary of state, James Madison, which would force Madison to deliver that commission.

SCOTUS Decision

Chief Justice John Marshall ruled that yes, it was indeed illegal for Madison to refuse to give Marbury his commission. And they wanted to give him the job. But they couldn't do it in this case, because the part of the 1789 Judiciary Act that expanded the Court's jurisdiction to include cases like this was unconstitutional. Marbury never got to put on the robe.

Why It Matters

This is the granddaddy of all Supreme Court cases to come, because it established judicial review, the power of the Supreme Court to hear cases on the constitutionality of laws. Which wasn't explicitly what the framers intended! However, this decision wasn't met with cheers and bells ringing and citizens crying, "Huzzah for Marshall! *Marbury v. Madison* has just established judicial review!" At the time, it came and went without much comment, and it would be over fifty years before the court again found a law to be unconstitutional.[3]

---

[2] This is a fiction of course, but nobody knows what Jefferson did with those commissions. Some hypothesize he chucked them into the fire.

[3] This was *Scott v. Sandford*, which we cover in the anticanon section.

MCCULLOCH V. MARYLAND

Decided in 1819: The government has powers that aren't in the Constitution, and the federal government reigns supreme—states cannot interfere with constitutional federal actions.

The Case

During the depression of 1818, states were hard up. Looking for cash, Maryland imposed a tax on all banks in the state that were not *chartered* in the state. The Second Bank of the United States, chartered in 1816, was the only bank not chartered in Maryland. When taxed, the national bank refused to pay, so Maryland took the cashier in charge, James William McCulloch, to court. It ended up in the Maryland Court of Appeals. The state argued that because the Constitution was mum on the subject of banks, the national government did not have the power to create its own bank at all. In other words, the action's not being enumerated in the Constitution meant that the action was unconstitutional. The Court of Appeals upheld Maryland, and the case was appealed to the Supreme Court.

SCOTUS Decision

The Court ruled unanimously that the Second Bank of the United States was constitutional and that the tax Maryland imposed was unconstitutional. In his opinion, Chief Justice John Marshall wrote that the Necessary and Proper Clause of the Constitution empowered Congress to take actions (such as the establishment of a national bank that serves the Congressional power to tax and regulate interstate commerce) that further the objectives of their enumerated powers. In other words, if it helps them do what they can and must explicitly do, then it's fair game. As far as Maryland's tax went, Marshall deemed this unconstitutional because it interfered with the federal government's dealings. Arguing that because "the power to tax involves the power to destroy," Maryland's tax undermined federal law's supremacy as mandated by the Constitution's Supremacy Clause.

Why It Matters

This ruling established implied Congressional powers, thereby clarifying the scope of the U.S. government's capacity. It also clarified the relationship between the states and the federal government by placing a prohibition on state behavior. If a state takes an action that in any way interferes with the superior law of the federal government, it is unconstitutional. Before *McCulloch v. Maryland,* the U.S. legislature's reach was unclear. After, the path was cleared for a strong federal government. Is that FDR we see in the distance?

MINERSVILLE V. GOBITIS AND
WEST VIRGINIA V. BARNETTE
———

Decided in 1940 and 1943 respectively: Refraining from saying the Pledge of Allegiance is not protected under the First Amendment. And then it is.

The Case

This is the only duo we have in here, and it's because it's one of the fastest reversals in Supreme Court history. In 1938, Walter

Gobitas,[4] a Jehovah's Witness, instructed his children to refrain from pledging allegiance to the flag at school.[5] The Gobitas family was summarily expelled. Likewise, in 1942, Marie and Gathie Barnett,[6] also Jehovah's Witnesses, refused to say the pledge in West Virginia and were expelled for "insubordination."

SCOTUS Ruling

In 1940, the court ruled eight to one that schools mandating a pledge or salute to the flag were not violating the First Amendment. Justice Felix Frankfurter wrote in the opinion that "national cohesion" was paramount, and the salute to the flag advanced that cohesion. But a scant three years later, in *West Virginia v. Barnette,* the court ruled six to three that saluting the flag was a "form of utterance" and therefore protected under the First Amendment, overruling *Minersville* completely. Justice Robert Jackson wrote the opinion,[7] which was announced on Flag Day.

---

[4] Okay, so the family name is Gobitas, but the court misspelled it Gobitis. And so it remains.

[5] There is a long history of Jehovah's Witnesses refusing to pledge fealty to any nation, as they view the Kingdom of Heaven as a government, and it would be treasonous to swear their loyalties anywhere else.

[6] You're not going to believe this, but the family name is actually Barnett and the court misspelled it as Barnette *and so it remains.*

[7] Including the famous passage: "If there is any fixed star in our constitutional constellation, it is that no official, high or petty, can prescribe what shall be orthodox in politics, nationalism, religion, or other matters of opinion or force citizens to confess by word or act their faith therein."

Why It Matters

One of the most fascinating aspects of these cases is how they related to public sentiment. After the *Gobitis* decision was announced, there were scores of attacks on Jehovah's Witnesses nationwide. One sheriff told reporters that the court's decision *justified* this violence, saying, "They're traitors; the Supreme Court says so. Ain't you heard?" However, by 1943, Americans had started to hear other stories of flag protest; Jehovah's Witnesses in Germany refusing to salute the Nazi flag and being sent to concentration camps.

MAPP V. OHIO

Decided in 1961: A state court cannot admit evidence that has been obtained unconstitutionally.

The Case

In 1957, Cleveland police were looking for a suspect potentially involved in a bombing at the house of Don King.[8] They believed the suspect was in the home of Dollree Mapp, and three officers showed up at her door. Mapp refused them entry unless they had a warrant. One officer waved a piece of paper in front of her and claimed it was a warrant, and Ms. Mapp took it from him to read. The police officers followed her into the house, took the paper back, and proceeded to search for the suspect. They found him (though eventually he was found innocent of all involvement in the bombing) and then continued to search

---

[8] Yep, that Don King. Before he was a famed boxing promoter, King worked as a numbers runner in Ohio.

Ms. Mapp's entire apartment. The police found a nude sketch and some "obscene" literature,[9] which was enough to convict her under Ohio's obscenity law. Ms. Mapp was sentenced for up to seven years. The police later admitted they never had obtained a warrant for her apartment, but Ohio had no laws preventing the use of evidence that had been gained illegally.

SCOTUS Decision
The court unanimously declared the antiquated obscenity statute in Ohio as unconstitutional. But far more importantly, in a six to three decision in favor of Ms. Mapp, the court ruled that evidence that was obtained in violation of Fourth Amendment search and seizure rights could not be used in a state court.

Why It Matters
Not being able to use evidence that had been obtained illegally is referred to as the "exclusionary rule," and it has many exceptions.[10] Federal courts operated under this rule since 1914, but this decision mandated that **state** courts, via incorporation from the Fourteenth Amendment, follow the same rules when it comes to evidence. Justice Tom C. Clark, in his opinion, wrote that "the State, by admitting evidence unlawfully seized, serves to encourage disobedience to the Federal Constitution which it is bound to uphold."

---

[9] Titles included *Memoirs of a Hotel Man* and *Affairs of a Troubadour.*

[10] E.g., frisking, the plain view exception, the good faith exception, and even an automobile exception!

ENGLE V. VITALE

Decided in 1962: A state cannot hold prayers in public schools.

The Case

The New York State Board of Regents authorized a nondenominational prayer that students had the option of reciting along with the Pledge of Allegiance at the start of school every morning. It went like this: "Almighty God, we acknowledge our dependence upon Thee, and we beg Thy blessings upon us, our parents, our teachers, and our country. Amen." Students had the option of begging out if they wanted, but a group of parents took issue with the prayer nonetheless. They argued that it violated the Establishment Clause of the First Amendment. Proponents of the prayer argued that it was constitutional on the basis of its being optional *and* religious-adjacent, also citing the First Amendment as justification. A coalition of parents, Jewish groups, and the American Civil Liberties Union sued the school board president and lost in the New York Court of Appeals. So they asked the Supreme Court to take it up.

> **CONSTITUTION 101:** The First Amendment of the Bill of Rights, the one that we think of as being all about free speech, in fact starts off by addressing religion: "Congress shall make no law respecting an establishment of religion," meaning that Congress is hereby ordered to stay out of it when it comes to all things Godlike. The second part of the First Amendment also deals with religion: "or prohibiting the free exercise thereof"; Congress is prohibited from passing a law that stops anyone from the free exercise of religion.

SCOTUS Decision

In a six-to-one ruling with two justices abstaining, the court ruled that a state-drafted school prayer was in violation of the Establishment Clause, regardless of whether students had the option of abstaining. Justice Hugo Black wrote the opinion and argued that prayer was by nature a religious act, specifically denominational or not. He cited America's constitutional separation of church and state and gave a long history of the fight for this separation dating back to sixteenth-century England. He wrote, "Our Founders were no more willing to let the content of their prayers and their privilege of praying whenever they pleased be influenced by the ballot box than they were to let these vital matters of personal conscience depend upon the succession of monarchs."

Why It Matters

This was the first in a series of Supreme Court cases that ruled to limit government-sponsored religious activity in schools. The idea is not to ban students from praying in schools—there is no prohibition on a student's choosing to engage in prayer so long as they do not interfere with the rights of others. Instead, this is a case about upholding the liberty of the individual over direction from the government.

TINKER V. DES MOINES

Decided in 1969: The First Amendment applies to students.

The Case

In 1965, thirteen-year-old Mary Beth Tinker, along with her brother John and several others, wore black armbands to school to mourn the dead on both sides of the Vietnam War, and also to show support for a Christmas truce. The Des Moines school board had gotten wind that this would occur and placed a pre-emptive ban on black armbands. The Tinkers wore them anyway, and were suspended.

SCOTUS Decision

The court ruled seven to two that the Tinkers' First Amendment rights had been violated. Justice Abe Fortas, who wrote the opinion, said that students and teachers do not "shed their constitutional rights to freedom of speech or expression at the schoolhouse gate." Only speech that can be proven disruptive justifies suppression. Justice Hugo Black, dissenting, cautioned that this decision was ushering in a "new revolutionary era of permissiveness."

Why It Matters

Because Justice Black wasn't wrong! It *did* usher in a revolutionary era of permissiveness. Students continue to be involved politically in the United States. This decision upheld the notion that they are people, they have a voice. Mary Beth to this day travels the country to tell her story and to inspire students to make themselves heard. Of course, as the years progressed, the "Tinker standard" of disruption would be redefined, but it remains the seminal student First Amendment rights case.

> **JUDICIAL BRANCH 101:** In *Bethel v. Fraser* the court ruled in favor of suppressing lewd or vulgar speech; in *Hazelwood v. Kuhlmeier,* it supported the censoring of articles about teen pregnancy in a school newspaper; and in *Morse v. Frederick,*

> it upheld that speech referencing drugs was disruptive. The
> speech in this instance was a wonderfully cryptic banner that
> read "Bong Hits 4 Jesus."

ROE V. WADE

Decided in 1973: A pregnant woman has the right to choose an abortion, and government restriction is limited.

The Case

Norma McCorvey, a woman in her first trimester of pregnancy (filing under the pseudonym Jane Roe), sued her district attorney, challenging the constitutionality of Texas's ban on all abortion unless to save the mother's life. Roe's lawyers argued that the law violated Roe's right to privacy under the First, Fourth, Fifth, Ninth, and Fourteenth Amendments. The U.S. District Court for the Northern District of Texas ruled in Roe's favor saying that the prohibition was, in fact, unconstitutional and granting her the right to an abortion. Texas took the case to the Supreme Court, which agreed to add it to the docket.

SCOTUS Decision

In a seven to two decision, the court ruled that a woman's right to choose to have an abortion was protected by her constitutional right to privacy, which could not be undermined by state law per the Due Process Clause of the Fourteenth Amendment.

> **CONSTITUTION 101:** The Fourteenth Amendment, Section 1,
> says, "No State shall make or enforce any law which shall
> abridge the privileges or immunities of citizens of the United
> States; nor shall any State deprive any person of life, liberty,

> or property, without due process of law." In the 1965 case *Griswald v. Connecticut,* the court established the notion of a "penumbra," a soft shadow, of rights within the Constitution. In the same way *McCulloch v. Maryland* established implied powers of Congress, *Griswald v. Connecticut* established implied rights of the individual. In that case, it was determined that the Bill of Rights grants us, to a certain degree, a right to privacy despite the fact that privacy is never explicitly addressed in the Constitution. So, under the Fourteenth Amendment, states had to abide by that implied right to privacy.

The court acknowledged that the state may have an interest in the health of the woman and in the "potentiality of human life," but that in the first trimester, the woman's right to privacy outranks that interest. In the second trimester, however, the state is permitted to regulate abortions when it comes to the health of the woman. In the third, the state may prohibit them outright *unless* the abortion would preserve the health or life of the mother.

Why It Matters

This case remains at the center of one of the most divisive debates in American politics and religion. It turned an often illegal, dangerous, and occasionally deadly procedure into one that is mostly safe and regulated. It cemented a woman's right to make decisions about her own body up to a point and extended the notion of privacy to abortion rights. At the same time, the decision in this case upheld a state's interest in maintaining order by permitting regulation and prohibition at later stages of a woman's pregnancy.

UNITED STATES V. NIXON

Decided in 1974: Executive privilege does *exist, but it does not mean that the president of the United States is immune from judicial processes under all circumstances.*

EXECUTIVE BRANCH 101: Executive privilege is never explicitly mentioned in the Constitution, but it has been invoked from our first president onward. It's the principle that the president of the United States and other members of the executive branch have the right to withhold information from Congress, courts, and the American public if that information pertains to national security or it is in the public interest to withhold White House deliberations. This includes the refusal of subpoenas. Executive privilege is considered an implied power of the executive branch related to the separation of powers in Article II of the Constitution. Basically, this is the executive branch's way of tempering the power that the legislative branch holds over it.

The Case

In the shadow of the Watergate Scandal,[11] special prosecutor Leon Jaworski sought to obtain tapes that President Nixon made of

---

[11] In the wee hours of June 17, 1972, five men were arrested while burglarizing the offices of the Democratic National Committee headquarters in the Watergate Building in Washington, D.C. The men, who would later be identified as being connected to Nixon's reelection campaign, were caught stealing documents and wiretapping phones. The attorney general appointed a special prosecutor to investigate the burglary, and over the course of the investigation it came to light that Nixon had recordings of phone calls believed to be related to the conspiracy. By the way, crackerjack reporters Bob Woodward and Carl Bernstein investigated the heck out of the story and exposed Nixon's connection to the burglary. Turns out it had been fueled by money from a slush fund for Nixon's reelection, and Nixon was trying to cover that up.

phone calls from the Oval Office following the indictment of the five Watergate burglars and two former CIA officers related to the crime. These tapes were believed to contain damning evidence against the indicted men and possibly against the president himself. Jaworski subpoenaed the tapes and Nixon refused to turn them over, claiming immunity under executive privilege. Nixon's attorney requested that U.S. District Court Judge John Sirica void the subpoena, Sirica refused and Nixon appealed directly to the Supreme Court.

SCOTUS Decision

In an eight-to-zero decision, with Judge William Rehnquist recusing himself due to connections to several of the men indicted in the Watergate case, the court ruled that Nixon must hand over the tapes. In a decision coauthored by several of the justices (to the chagrin of Chief Justice Warren E. Burger), the court decided that though executive privilege existed in regards to certain military and diplomatic issues, the executive branch did not have absolute privilege to withhold information when it came to the demands of due process of law and the administration of justice.

Why It Matters

This decision resulted in the release of the Watergate tapes and the resignation of President Nixon, who was at the time the subject of impeachment proceedings in the House of Representatives. It effectively put the final nail in the coffin of Nixon's presidency and defined and limited the doctrine of executive privilege. This case affirmed that the president may indeed, for the good of the nation, need to claim confidentiality in certain matters. But when it comes to the pursuit of justice in a criminal trial, a general desire for confidentiality is not sufficient grounds for denying a subpoena.

NEW JERSEY V. TLO

Decided in 1985: Students do not have the same protections under the Fourth Amendment within a school setting as they do when outside that setting.

The Case

A student referred to as TLO was caught smoking cigarettes in the girls' bathroom. When she was brought to a school administrator, she denied any such thing. She was asked to open her purse, which she refused. The administrator searched her purse regardless, finding the offending pack of cigarettes as well as some rolling papers. He then, suspecting marijuana use, searched the purse even further, discovering a bag of pot, a large roll of cash, some empty plastic baggies, and a list of students who owed TLO money. She was brought to the police station and confessed she had been dealing marijuana. Her lawyer argued that the initial search of the purse was unconstitutional, and via the exclusionary rule, all evidence gathered later was also inadmissible, including her confession.[12]

SCOTUS Ruling

The court ruled six to three that the search of TLO's purse did not violate the Fourth Amendment. Justice Byron White wrote

---

[12] The term for this, evidence gathered subsequent to other evidence gathered illegally, is the lovely "fruit from a poisonous tree."

in the opinion that it would be unreasonable "that the full panoply of constitutional rules applies with the same force and effect in the schoolhouse as it does in the enforcement of criminal laws." An adult citizen or a juvenile not in school cannot have their possessions searched without "probable cause," but, as Justice Brennan cautioned in his concurring opinion, TLO ruled that searching a student in school only required a "reasonableness" standard.

Why It Matters

Time and again we see that the need to protect students and support a successful learning environment comes into conflict with constitutional rights. Sometimes, like in *Tinker v. Des Moines,* the law comes down in favor of the rights of the student. And in others, like *TLO,* it falls on the side of the school maintaining order and discipline.

TEXAS V. JOHNSON

Decided in 1989: The burning of a U.S. flag is protected speech under the First Amendment.

The Case

While protesting the Republican National Convention in Dallas in 1984, Gregory Lee "Joey" Johnson poured kerosene onto a U.S. flag and set it on fire. He was fined $2,000 and sentenced to a year in prison for "desecrating a venerable object." He appealed to the Texas Court of Criminal Appeals and the decision was reversed. Texas petitioned for the Supreme Court to hear the case.

SCOTUS Ruling

In a narrow five-to-four decision, the court ruled that the burning of a flag can indeed be considered speech,[13] and Johnson's act was distinctly political in nature, and therefore was protected under the First Amendment. Justice William Brennan, who wrote the opinion, stated, "We do not consecrate the flag by punishing its desecration, for in doing so we dilute the freedom that this cherished emblem represents." Justices White, O'Connor, and Rehnquist, in their dissent, said, "The flag is not simply another 'idea' or 'point of view.'" They then quoted numerous battles, monuments, and flag-centric poems and songs.

Why It Matters

This decision pushes at the corners of our First Amendment liberties. To some, the flag is sacrosanct, and its desecration outside the boundaries of protest. To others, allowing the burning of the flag is the ultimate representation of our freedom. At the time of this decision, forty-eight states had laws prohibiting abusing the flag. In 1995, the Flag Desecration Amendment[14] passed the House and died in the Senate, a process that would be repeated six times. In 2006, it lost in the Senate by a single vote. Regardless of where you stand, it is clear that this debate is not yet over, despite what the Supreme Court says.

---

[13] The Court's reasoning is that the freedom of speech adheres to the message being communicated, not the method by which it is communicated. So a dance, a painting, and a Facebook like (as of 2013) are protected speech if their message is clear. And it doesn't get much clearer than a burning flag.

[14] Which consists entirely of these words: "The Congress shall have power to prohibit the physical desecration of the flag of the United States."

CITIZENS UNITED V. FEC

Decided in 2010: Prohibiting corporations and unions from using their general treasury funds to finance political ads violates the First Amendment.

The Case

The conservative nonprofit organization Citizens United made a film critical of Hillary Clinton and wanted to air it shortly before the 2008 Presidential Election. This would be in violation of the Bipartisan Campaign Reform Act which, among other provisions, prohibits corporations (including nonprofits) from airing ads that name a federal candidate within thirty days of a primary and sixty days of a general election. In December of 2007, Citizens United filed a complaint in U.S. District Court for D.C. asking the court to declare certain prohibitions around "electioneering communications" to be unconstitutional. The court denied the motion, so Citizens United appealed to the Supreme Court.

SCOTUS Decision

The court ruled in a five-to-four decision that the First Amendment prohibits the government from restricting independent expenditures—that is, a campaign communication (television ad, leaflet, etc.) advocating for or against a candidate that is not made in partnership with that candidate—for corporations, including nonprofits and unions. The majority argued that political speech, regardless of whether it was from an individual or a corporation, was vital to American democracy. The court did, however, uphold the BCRA's ban on direct campaign contributions from corporations to candidates and its disclosure requirements.

Why It Matters

Citizens United, along with a number of similar cases that followed, is basically the reason we have Super PACS. This ruling freed up corporations and labor unions to spend unlimited funds in campaigning for or against a candidate. Since the controversial ruling, there have been calls for a constitutional amendment to abolish the legal notion of corporate personhood. This is the notion, reinforced by several SCOTUS cases, that a corporation has some of the rights of an individual human being.

15

ANTICANON: FOUR BAD SUPREME COURT DECISIONS

The word has a kind of dark pall, doesn't it? *Anticanon.* Something that went wrong and goes on echoing in our ears. In the legal system, this is the term for cases that are now considered to have been wrongly decided. When it comes to the Supreme Court, as you might imagine, the wrong decision can have hideous consequences. And indeed these decisions did.

DRED SCOTT V. SANFORD

Decided in 1857: Black Americans, enslaved or not, are not citizens of the United States. They cannot sue in federal court and are not privy to the other rights and privileges of citizenship. Furthermore, the Court does not have the power to ban slavery in U.S. territories, and the rights of slaveholders are protected under the Fifth Amendment because enslaved people are considered property.

The Case

Dred Scott was an enslaved man purchased by a Dr. John Emerson and moved to Illinois and later Wisconsin territory, both of which prohibited slavery. Over the next ten years, Dr. Emerson hired Scott, and later Scott's wife, Harriet Robinson, out to others in violation of the Missouri Compromise, Northwest Ordinance, and Wisconsin Enabling Act, all of which prohibited the institution of slavery in those states and territories. After Emerson died in 1843, his wife, Eliza, inherited his property, which included Scott and his family. In 1846, Scott attempted to purchase his freedom from Eliza. She refused, and Scott filed for freedom in a Missouri court. His argument was that their prior residence in a free state made his wife and him free individuals, and that their child was free due to having been born on a steamboat between a free state and a free territory. Scott lost this case on a technicality—he failed to prove that he was owned by Emerson's widow. Scott appealed, and the jury ruled in his favor. However, Emerson would not lose her enslaved, and appealed this decision. The courts ruled in her favor, deciding that the Scotts should have sued for freedom while actually in a free state. Now in Missouri, it was too late. Scott appealed to the federal courts, and the case ended up before the Supreme Court. At this point, Scott and his family had been transferred to Eliza Emerson's brother, John Sanford. Sanford argued that no person of African descent or descended from slaves could be a citizen, as defined in Article III of the Constitution.

SCOTUS Decision

The Court agreed with Sanford. In a seven-to-two decision, the majority held that any "negro," regardless of their status as enslaved or free, who was descended from people who were brought into the U.S. and enslaved, could not be a citizen of the United States. If Scott wasn't a citizen, Chief Justice Roger Taney reasoned, in his opinion, he could not sue in federal court. If he could not sue in federal court, the Supreme Court had no jurisdiction in his case. Taney also deemed the Missouri Compromise, which admitted Missouri as a slave state and Maine as a free state, unconstitutional because Congress did not have the power to prohibit slavery in the territories. He also ruled that because enslaved people were property, their owners' rights were protected in the Fifth Amendment.

> **JUDICIAL BRANCH 101:** In his dissent, Justice Robbins Curtis argued that Taney should have stopped at the jurisdiction argument—if the court had no jurisdiction in the case because Scott was not a citizen, then why go on to make rulings on the constitutionality of the Missouri Compromise and the rights of slave owners? Justice John McLean agreed and added that people descended from enslaved individuals could, in fact, be citizens because they had the right to vote in five states already.

Why It Matters

The public reaction to this decision was vitriolic in the North and celebratory in the South. It was viewed as a victory for southern slave-owning states, and for Northern Republicans it was a sign of conspiracy to expand slavery throughout the territories and eventually legalize the institution the nation over. President

James Buchanan, who learned of the verdict in advance, considered this a great win, cementing slavery under the purview of the states. But in a nation already deeply divided over the issue, the Dred Scott decision fanned the flames that would set the country ablaze in the Civil War. The decision divided the Democratic Party and helped to cement the Republican platform in the 1860 election and secure Abraham Lincoln the presidency. The decision was effectively overturned by passage of the Thirteenth (abolishment of slavery) and Fourteenth (formerly enslaved people are citizens and have equal protection under the Constitution) Amendments during the Reconstruction Era, but remains a consistently cited example of a weak constitutional interpretation that forever tarnished the Supreme Court.

Ownership of Dred Scott and his family was transferred to the family of Scott's original enslaver, Peter Blow. Blow's son Taylor filed manumission papers for the Scotts in 1857. Dred Scott died just over a year after obtaining the freedom he'd fought for for over a decade.

PLESSY V. FERGUSON

Decided in 1896: Racial segregation is legal under the "separate but equal" doctrine.

The Case

In 1890, Louisiana passed the Separate Car Act, requiring all in-state railroads to provide "separate but equal" railcars for white and Black passengers. Passengers were barred from entering the railcar that did not reflect their race. A year later, a group of concerned Creole activists in New Orleans formed the Citizens' Committee to Test the Constitutionality of the Separate Car Law. They theorized that the law was ultimately unenforceable because it did not define "colored" and "white." They chose Homer Plessy, a man who was one-eighth Black, to test the theory. Plessy purchased a ticket for, and sat in, the white section of the train. He was asked to move, refused to, and was arrested. At trial, Plessy's lawyers contended that the Separate Car Act was unconstitutional and in violation of the Thirteenth and Fourteenth Amendments. Judge John H. Ferguson dismissed the claim. The state supreme court upheld Ferguson's ruling, so Plessy appealed to the federal Supreme Court.

SCOTUS Decision

In a seven-to-one decision, with Justice Josiah Brewer abstaining, the Supreme Court upheld the lower courts' decision. Justice Henry Billings Brown wrote the opinion, arguing that the Separate Car Act was constitutional. Addressing the constitutional rights violations argued by Plessy's lawyer, Brewer asserted first that the Act was not in violation of the Thirteenth Amendment as it did not reestablish slavery or result in a badge of slavery. To Plessy's claim that the Act resulted in a label of inferiority, Brewer wrote, "If this be so, it is not by reason of anything found in the act, but solely because the colored race chooses to put that construction upon it." In other words, if this Act makes you feel discriminated against, that's your own fault. On the Fourteenth Amendment argument, Brewer ruled that the Equal Protection Clause remained unchallenged. His reasoning was that the

Fourteenth only guaranteed legal equality between white and Black Americans, not social equality. Because the Act required "equal" accommodations for both white and Black Americans, Brewer argued, it did not violate a person's right to equal protection. Social equality—i.e., being able to choose which train car you want to sit in—did not fall under the protective umbrella of the Constitution. Brewer, peach of a man, put it like this: "if one race be inferior to the other socially, the constitution of the United States cannot put them upon the same plane."

> **JUDICIAL BRANCH 101:** Plessy's lawyer argued that the segregation of the Separate Car Act violated the Equal Protection Clause of the Fourteenth Amendment, which reads, "No State shall [. . .] deny to any person within its jurisdiction the equal protection of the laws." By prohibiting Black Americans from sitting in white cars and vice versa, Plessy's lawyer argued, the law inherently denied equal treatment under constitutional law. He wasn't wrong, folks.

The lone dissenter was Justice John Marshall Harlan, who called the Constitution "colorblind," pointed out something truly obvious—that the Thirteenth and Fourteenth Amendments were intended to provide true equality in the United States, regardless of race. Similarly calling bull, he wrote that the Separate Car Act was *of course* designed to subjugate Black individuals, and in doing so impose a badge of servitude. The United States, he contended, had no class system. "The judgment this day rendered will," Harlan wrote, "in time, prove to be quite as pernicious as the decision made by this tribunal in the Dred Scott Case."

Why It Matters

Harlan was, of course, correct. This ruling resulted in an implicit go-ahead for racial segregation for decades to come in the United States. It created a de facto caste system and precluded legal challenges to segregation on the basis of race well into the twentieth century. It is due to this ruling that "separate but equal" prevailed and the Jim Crow South thrived. In a case that ought to have been a step toward solidifying the rights established by the Reconstruction Amendments, *Plessy v. Ferguson* instead paved the way for a half-century of blatant racial segregation, injustice, and violence.

LOCHNER V. NEW YORK

Decided in 1905: State law setting maximum working hours is unconstitutional, in violation of the freedom of contract between employer and employee guaranteed by the Fourteenth Amendment.

The Case

New York State passed the Bakeshop Act in 1897—a labor law that in part prohibited "biscuit, bread, cake, and confectionary establishment" employees from working more than sixty hours per week. Joseph Lochner, proprietor of Utica's own Lochner Home Bakery, allowed an employee to work more than sixty hours a week and was fined fifty dollars. He was to be incarcerated until he coughed it up, up to fifty days. Lochner challenged the ruling first in the New York Court of Appeals, which upheld it, and then to the Supreme Court.

SCOTUS Decision

In a five-to-four decision, the court ruled in Lochner's favor and found the Bakeshop Act unconstitutional. New York state, and in fact *any* state, wrote Justice Rufus Peckham in his opinion, was prohibited from interfering with employment contracts for the most part. Citing the Due Process Clause of the Fourteenth Amendment, the majority argued that the right to buy and sell labor through contract constituted an individual liberty. Therefore, any act attempting to regulate this liberty is in violation of the "life, liberty, and property" rights guaranteed by the Fourteenth. The court allowed for a state occasionally wielding its police powers in order to enforce its citizens' safety, in the case of, say, dangerous mining conditions, but reasoned that baking was a relatively safe occupation and so the Act had no teeth. This is where we get the notion of "substantive due process." To understand what that means, we have to go over the difference between substantive and procedural due process, which is tricky indeed. Procedural due process, "due process under law," of the Fourteenth Amendment means that a government must follow fair procedures before depriving an individual of life, liberty, or property. Pretty straightforward—procedural due process is about the procedure of impeding rights. Substantive due process, on the other hand, is considerably more elusive. This concept has not been properly, explicitly defined by the Supreme Court, and indeed there are justices and law scholars who would argue that the principle does not actually exist. Substantive due process is about Constitutional rights themselves, and whether a government has just cause to impede upon them. This doctrine holds that there are rights guaranteed us by the Constitution that cannot be impeded without sufficient cause, regardless of **how** they are impeded. In order to uphold the Lochner decision by way of the Constitution, the concept of substantive due process (does New York state have sufficient cause to impose regulation on the bakeshop industry?) was necessary. This is in part because though SCOTUS precedent had determined that the Due Process Clause protects the right to contract (*Allgeyer v. Louisiana*, 1897), it had also determined that the right to contract was not absolute and was subject to state police powers at a point. To determine whether those police powers are wielded legitimately, we operate under the doctrine of substantive due process. Whew. Got that? Us neither.

The majority faced two dissents, one from Justice John Marshall Harlan (remember him from *Plessy v. Ferguson*? Yeah, he's still looking out), who opined that state labor regulation did indeed fall under their police powers so long as the state could reasonably prove that an act was protecting public health or morals. Given the prevalence of respiratory problems reported by bakeshop workers, he asserted, the New York Act could reasonably prove just that. Justice Oliver Wendell Holmes, Jr., in a mic drop that went down as one of the most influential in SCOTUS history, argued that the majority was making a ruling based on personal opinion and not the content of the Constitution itself. He wrote, "a constitution is not intended to embody a particular economic theory, whether of paternalism and the organic relation of the citizen to the State or of laissez faire."[1] In other

---

[1] A fun French name for an economic system in which the government does not interfere with transactions between two private parties.

words, how in thundering tarnation are you getting "freedom of contract" out of the protection of "life, liberty, or property"? This economic theory, he asserted, was one which the country itself by and large "does not entertain."

Why It Matters

For three decades after Lochner, the Supreme Court stuck to its guns and tended to rule against states attempting to regulate their labor market. A number of justices operated fairly explicitly according to a belief in *laissez-faire* economics. These thirty years are actually referred to as the Lochner Era, and involved the shooting down of state attempts at minimum wage laws and contracts that forbid employees from entering unions. It wasn't until the mid-1930s that the court ruled that freedom of contract is *not* actually implicit in the Constitution, and should not be absolutely unrestricted. The doctrine of substantive due process remained, but is applied more stringently to cases of personal, rather than economic, liberties.

KOREMATSU V. UNITED STATES

Decided in 1944: The order commanding all people of Japanese descent to be excluded from designated "military areas" and forcibly relocated is constitutional under the Fourteenth Amendment.

The Case

On February 19, 1942, just over two months after the attack on Pearl Harbor and the U.S. joining World War II, President Franklin Delano Roosevelt issued Executive Order 9066. This order authorized the secretary of war and his commanders to designate "military areas [. . .] from which any and all persons may be excluded." Though this order did not explicitly identify people of Japanese descent, it de facto resulted in the forced relocation of over a hundred thousand Japanese and Japanese Americans to internment camps scattered across the United States. Fred Korematsu, a Japanese American living in what became a designated "military area," refused to go. He was arrested and convicted, then challenged his conviction on the grounds that the order violated the Fifth Amendment. A court of appeals upheld Korematsu's conviction, and he appealed to the Supreme Court.

SCOTUS Decision

In a six-to-three decision, the majority upheld Korematsu's conviction and ruled the exclusion order constitutional. Justice Hugo Black wrote the decision, saying plainly that the exclusion order was not based on personal or racial hostility, but because the United States was at war with the Japanese Empire and therefore had reasonable cause to take measures to preserve national security. Though the court acknowledged that stripping the civil rights of a single racial group was "immediately suspect," because this particular military action did not reflect racial hostility, but rather an inability to quickly sort out the loyal Japanese Americans from the disloyal, the compulsory batch relocation of thousands was not unconstitutional. The court did not directly address the incarceration of thousands of citizens without due process.

Justice Frank Murphy's dissent explicitly called the decision out for the legalization of racism and the denial of unalienable rights to citizens of the United States. Justice Josephus Roberts wrote that Korematsu was being punished "for not submitting to imprisonment in a concentration camp, based on his ancestry, and solely because of his ancestry, without evidence or inquiry concerning his loyalty and good disposition towards the United States." Justice Robert Jackson warned against cementing a temporary military order within the Constitution, "the Court for all time has validated the principle of racial discrimination in criminal procedure and of transplanting American citizens."

Why It Matters

This decision resulted in a widespread *mea maxima culpa* at the federal level, first with a 1980 Congressional Commission calling the Korematsu decision effectively overruled, then with Korematsu's own appeal in 1983, which resulted in an official voiding of the conviction, though not a voiding of the precedent set by the case. The Civil Liberties Act of 1988 then granted reparations to those Japanese Americans interred in relocation camps during World War II. It was not until 2018, however, during the ruling on *Trump v. Hawaii*, that Chief Justice John Roberts called *Korematsu* "gravely wrong the day it was decided [. . .] and—to be clear—has no place in law under the Constitution," thereby declaring unlawful the forcible relocation of U.S. citizens to concentration camps solely on the basis of race.

JUDICIAL BRANCH 101: In September 2017, President Donald J. Trump signed Presidential Proclamation 9645, which restricted the travel of people from a number of predominantly Muslim nations into the United States, as well as refugees who did not have certain travel documents. Several states, including Hawaii, challenged these restrictions on the grounds that they constituted a ban on people of a certain religion entering the country. Lower courts did not address the constitutionality of the issue, but determined that the plaintiffs had a good chance of winning this case if arguing on the freedom of religion clause of the First Amendment and the Immigration and Nationality Act. The Supreme Court then reversed that ruling, deferring to the executive branch and determining that the plaintiff did not, in fact, stand a good chance of success arguing either point. The case was then remanded to lower courts for further proceedings. Justice Sonia Sotomayor wrote the dissent, comparing the ruling to that in *Korematsu*.

A USER'S GUIDE

Carry this book with you on your forays into American government and you will carry your power and protection. We're not saying this thing will stop a long sword (and we're not saying it *wouldn't*), but it will allow you to wield your rights in order to live your most empowered, most engaged life here in these United States, if you so choose. You've got the background, you know how and why we got here and what's going on in the country today.

So now it's time to get your hands dirty. Or, perhaps, to rinse your hands clean by putting your money and actions where your mouth is. Let's make this reference guide a little more personal and put a plan together to make this country work for you.

16

HOW TO COMMUNICATE
WITH YOUR LEGISLATORS

The easiest, most direct way of getting in touch with your legislators is by calling their offices directly. Whatever issue has compelled you to call, be ready to speak to it clearly and directly. "I'm concerned about recycling practices in my state/ district/town and I would like Senator/Representative So-and-so to vote for a bill that addresses it."

When an assistant picks up, you'll be asked whether you require a response to your message—that one's up to you. Leave your name and zip code, get straight to the message, and sign off. The idea is to add your voice to the dozens, hundreds, thousands of others who are telling that legislator what they want. Remember, you are their constituent. They need you as much as you need them if they plan to keep their seat in office, so if enough voters demand legislative action, it's that much more likely to happen. Even if you aren't a voter *yet,* your voice will be compelling when added to the rest.

Now, here's where you need to do a little work. Use any search engine to look up your local, state, and federal representatives. All you need to know are your address and zip code to figure out what district you live in and who represents you.

If you have any intention of ever moving, you may want to use pencil.

I live in the _____ County District of _____ County, and the _____ Congressional District of the State of _____ .

City/Town Hall Phone Number:

State Representative Phone Number:

State Senator Phone Number:

Federal Representative Phone Number:

Federal Senators Phone Numbers:

White House Office of the President Phone Number: 202-456-1111

17

HOW TO LOBBY FOR WHAT YOU BELIEVE IN

Calling your representative is a great first step toward having your needs and wants met in this democracy—it's actually step one of lobbying, and the most simple, direct way to do it. But you don't have to stop there! There's nothing quite like a face-to-face, especially a face-to-face with a face that a legislator really wants to appeal to.[1] Here's how you get your face in front of their face.

---

[1] Consider this—do you represent a group that your legislator has been trying to gain the attention of? A voter bloc that they'll need to succeed in the next election? A demographic at the center of a piece of legislation they've been trying to pass? Use it, baby! This is politics, after all. And remember, kids are PR catnip. Are you a kid? Get yourself a meeting with your legislator and lay down the law. You have power.

1. PREPARE

You already know the issue that's getting your goat, but now's the time to refine your approach. You'll have limited time with your representative, so be ready with relevant points. Do you know when the vote is going down? Who the sponsors of a bill are? Who is lobbying against or for this issue? What about your legislator themselves—where do they tend to land on this issue? How have they voted in the past? What did they campaign on? Knowing the answers to these questions will help you craft your best argument in favor of or against legislation.

2. MAKE AN APPOINTMENT

You can call your State House switchboard or the Federal Senate (202-224-3121) or House (202-225-3121) switchboard, or call the offices of your representative directly. Ask to speak to whoever makes the schedule or appointments for the legislator, and request a sit-down. There are a number of places this could go down—a state legislator's office in a state house, the state offices of a U.S. representative, the D.C. office of a U.S. rep, or some other location. Don't be surprised if you're only given ten minutes; these people have packed schedules. Tell the scheduler your name and what it is you're hoping to talk about. You may only get a meeting with a legislative assistant! That's okay. Take it.

3. MEET, GREET, ENTREAT

Show up a little early, dress nicely, come with collateral. You're going to want to leave the legislator with a fact sheet that reiterates your request, why it matters, whom it'll affect, etc. Start with a handshake, a "thanks for meeting with me," and a brief, direct rundown of why you're there. If you can share a personal story that backs up your legislative wants, that's gold. If it's relevant, it helps to know who else supports your issue so that you can name- and organization-drop while also emphasizing the strength of your position. And then you want to lay the pressure on at the very end. "Madame Senator, will you be voting 'no' on this bill?" Get a straight answer, and have a line or two prepared in case you need to change their mind.

4. WRITE A THANK-YOU LETTER

Yes, seriously. Use this letter to reiterate your point and to remind the legislator that they met with you. Also, you know what, civility is nice.

18

HOW TO STAGE A PROTEST

Taking the history of citizen-driven legislation as a whole, you'll notice a common theme. People got legislative attention when they banded together. When they took to the streets. When they refused to work, or even refused to eat. When they staged sit-ins and lie-ins and smash-all-the-bottles-starting-with-the-top-shelf-ins. Grassroots movements have a great deal of legislative sway, even if it takes decades to see the fruits of labor.

With limited restrictions, our first amendment right to free speech allows us to give voice to an issue we care about in the public sphere in the form of peaceful protest. So if you're tired of stewing at home, tired of complaining over the dinner table, tired of getting your heart smashed up by legislation or lack thereof, maybe it's time to take it to the streets.

1. DON'T GO IT ALONE.

You don't have to wait until you have a large coalition to plan your protest, but you're going to be a heck of a lot more successful if you do this in a group. Numbers signify support for an issue. The more of you there are, the greater the pressure will be on the legislators who are watching this all happen. Find your like-minded activists on social media, at town and city meetings, through local organizations, and suggest a time to meet, discuss your protest, and clarify your intention. Are you protesting animal testing by some cosmetics company down the street? Figure out the clearest messaging, determine whether you'll have a chant and whether you'll make signs or have uniforms or costumes to draw attention to yourselves.

2. PICK A LEADER.

Movements can fall apart without strong leadership. Identify the person in your ranks with the clearest sense of mission, the most commanding presence, the best organizational and rallying skills, and lift them up. It might be you, or it might be someone who joined things late in the game. Put the goal and the message above individual desires—maybe you started this thing, but someone else might be better at getting your protest over the finish line.

3. PICK A LOCATION.

In order for your protest to be legal, it has to be done in a public place. This means streets, sidewalks, parks, sometimes areas around government buildings. If you protest on private property, you're subject to the whims of the property owner. You'll have to abide by their rules and you can most certainly get kicked off. When it comes to choosing the location of your march, sit- or lie-in, symbolism can be some nice icing on the cake. Did a famous protest happen in this same location decades ago? Are you in clear view of the capitol building? Are you in or near the place where some injustice occurred that's related to your protest?

4. PICK A DATE.

There are two main and sometimes opposing objectives to consider when picking the date. Either your focus is on getting as many people out on the streets as possible or it's to ensure that the object of your protest sees it happen. In the case of the former, weekends are best. You're just going to get more people to show. But if it's that cosmetics company you need the attention of, you're probably looking at the middle of the day on a weekday.

5. FIGURE OUT WHETHER YOU NEED A PERMIT.

For the most part, the First Amendment protects your right to protest without use of a permit. However, if you're going to be messing with traffic, causing a lot of noise, or staging in an area that requires some kind of advance notice, like a park or City Hall plaza, there's a chance that your city or town can reasonably require you to obtain a permit. You'll usually need to obtain this weeks before the scheduled event, so look into this early! Because of the First Amendment, there are many opportunities for challenge of permit restrictions. Feel free to get a lawyer involved. And it may be prudent to notify the police either way in order to ensure crowd control and avoid spontaneous conflict.

6. TELL EVERYONE.

Because you've planned this weeks in advance, you'll have plenty of time to plaster social media, coffee shops, telephone poles, and newspapers with the details of your planned protest. Use this time to share relevant articles about related legislation and events. If Congress has just done something that fires you up, tell other people about it. Get them fired up. You never know when something will go down that'll drum up hundreds of people who want to voice their opposition or support at your side.

7. KNOW HOW IT'LL GO DOWN, AND BE SAFE.

Plan out the order of events with your fellow organizers. Know the route of the march, know when you want speeches to happen and who is going to give them, know how long your sit-in will last. Know your rights! Even if you don't have a permit, if your protest march obeys traffic laws and stays on the sidewalks, it's constitutional. Just make sure passers-by have space and aren't "physically or maliciously" detained by your group. Same goes for distributing pamphlets. You can't force anyone to take them, but you can offer them freely. Prepare your fellow protestors to be stopped, and possibly subjected to tear gas, pepper spray, rubber bullets, beatings, and arrests by police officers. Tell them to peacefully voice their First Amendment right to be doing what they're doing, and remind everyone that preserving their physical safety and life is paramount.

A note on non-peaceful protest: Though it is not protected action, and is likely prohibited wherever you are, looting and property damage have been objectively effective means of drawing attention to an issue and positively impacting policy change. Peaceful protest can do the same thing, a fact argued and proven out by Dr. Martin Luther King, Jr. and the thousands who participated in such protests during the Civil Rights movement. Both are true. This is not a condonation of violence, but an acknowledgment that this form of protest has often been used to great effect. It has also been used since before we were a nation, when dozens of men dressed as Native Americans dumped 342 chests of tea into Boston Harbor in protest of the British Tea Tax. John Adams called it "absolutely and indispensably" necessary.

You have the right—it's your very first one—to get loud about what you believe in.

But let's say you've gotten as loud as you possibly can, and they're still not listening? You've always got the last resort option in this nation of becoming *one of them.* Then they'll have to listen to you because the people put you in charge. Ready to discover the joys and frustrations of bureaucracy up close and personal?

19

HOW TO RUN FOR OFFICE

Remember how we told you the barrier for entry into the House, Senate, and *especially* the presidency is fairly high? And white? And wealthy? And connected?

That was awfully discouraging of us.

Truth is, it *is* hard to rise to the level of a legislator at the federal level. And leader of the free world? Yeah. Tough gig to snag. That said—it is *also* true that you *can* rise to that level. It sure helps to be born into money, privilege, and a world of fancy friends, but guess what? You can also go for it—and succeed—even if you don't have these things! This is America!

So where do you start, especially if you have none of those things? Local government, baby.

STEP 1: CAN YOU RUN?

We don't mean "do you have what it takes?" We mean "are you allowed?" Though you'll likely have to meet more stringent requirements than a candidate for the presidency, the qualifications shouldn't be terribly limiting. Check out your county or municipality elections website and figure out how old you have to be, how long you have to have lived in whatever region you're running in, and whether you need signatures or cash to get on the ballot (we'll get to that later). Make note of special requirements for roles like prosecuting attorney and sheriff. Some won't have any special requirements, but many will want you to actually be a lawyer or law enforcement officer, for example, to qualify for candidacy.

Oh, and by the way, you're usually going to need to be registered to vote. And if you aren't already, what are you even *doing*?

STEP 2: WHERE CAN YOU MAKE A DIFFERENCE?

It sounds a little schmaltzy, but if you're deliberating a run for office, you should look into those elected positions that pertain to some experience or expertise that you actually have. Been working as a park ranger for a while? Think Parks and Rec director. Are you a parent who's endlessly frustrated with your school district? Set your sights on that school board. Are you one heck of a committed, organized assistant? You might just shine as the clerk to end all clerks and ease the headache of paperwork down at the county courthouse.

You're going to be up against people with more resources and more knowhow, but it makes a difference if you actually care.

You'll work harder and smarter, and voters will be able to tell that you're in it for the right reasons.

STEP 3: GET YOUR PRIORITIES IN ORDER.

Okay, so you've identified the office that suits you best. Time to figure out whether you can sound like you know what you're talking about. If you want to run for mayor, identify what your city needs and the concrete ideas you have for attending to those needs. Are you a police officer making a run for sheriff? Great. How are you going to keep people safer than the sheriff in office right now? Gunning for auditor? Bold move, money brains. Do some intel work, figure out what's been slipping through the cracks in your county, and get ready to convince people you're going to know where every last cent of their tax dollars is going. Ask other citizens what they want, ask former, even current, elected officers what the job entails.

Now write a stump speech and practice it in front of your kid, your spouse, your dog. Refine it. Get the messaging down. Got it? Good. You're ready for the next step.

STEP 4: FIGURE OUT HOW MANY VOTES YOU NEED TO WIN.

You're going to build your campaign strategy around this number, and there's an actual mathematical formula to figure it out. Determine how many people turned out for the last three elections, then average that number and multiply it by the number of registered voters in your county, municipality, etc. That's the projected turnout for your election. Now divide that by two, add one, and that's your winning number!

STEP 5: MAKE A BUDGET.

If you know how many supporters you're going to need, you can start to determine what this run is gonna cost you. Garnering support will mean traveling around—that means gas, maybe even bus and airline tickets, the cost of lodging and food and coffee that'll keep you going when you want to throw in the towel. You'll (probably) need a staff. Now, maybe your daughter is well-equipped enough to help Mom out part time in her run for school board, but you might need to hire actual campaign staffers to help you out. You're going to need collateral, too, which in this case is the word we use to describe mailers, fliers, lawn signs, etc. Maybe you want to advertise, get your handsome mug up on the biggest billboard in town. Maybe you're aiming to film a campaign commercial or two—it all takes cash.

Before you start fundraising, there's one thing you *should* do, and one you really *must* do. The should is request campaign finance disclosures from past elections—this is the best way to project exactly how much green you're going to need. The must is familiarize yourself with campaign finance laws in your state. There's going to be a limit to how much you can legally raise, how much an individual can give you, and rules for how to disclose it all. After you do all this, open up an account in the campaign's name. This isn't *your* money, it's your campaign's money, and that's the only place you're allowed to spend it.

STEP 6: DETERMINE WHAT YOU NEED TO GET ON THE BALLOT.

There's always a deadline! There's often a fee! Sometimes you need to have enough signatures from people in the community!

Check in with your local board of elections or the county clerk's office.

STEP 7: FUNDRAISE!

If you've never asked total strangers—or worse, close friends—for money before, this is going to be weird for you. "I'm running for coroner and I need to raise $5,000 to do it, will you give me money so I can be the one to determine the causes of suspicious deaths in this podunk town?" is a *hard ask*. Just start with the people closest to you who are most likely to believe you when you say you believe in this run and you're the person for the job. Then branch out into the community. Throw a few parties. Tap your church, your intramural league, parents who are as frustrated with the school board as you are. The more people who donate, the more people who can be *convinced* to donate. And remember, the fundraising process is about more than just moolah, it's also about helping you to . . .

STEP 8: RECRUIT SUPPORTERS.

You've been telling family and friends that you need money. Tell them you need votes, too. And then tell them to tell their family and friends. Work that network. Get as many phone numbers and email addresses as you can. The easiest way to get voter info is to request the district voter list from the election commission.

Ask for fervent supporters to volunteer their time. Spend some of that hard-asked cash to hire staffers who are going to organize this effort and make calls, send out emails, design mailers and lawn signs, come up with your slogan, tap their own networks, and walk door to dang door with a big smile, a friendly pitch, and a simple question, "Can we count on your vote?"

Depending on the size of your campaign, you may want to invest in a proper campaign manager, maybe even a marketing guru of some kind, to up your chances of winning.

A major part of this push is going to be establishing your online presence. Make a website, make it pretty. Pictures of you engaged with the community, pictures of you doing a job that proves that you'll excel when elected, pictures of you with a puppy (for real). Have a donate button, have a calendar of events, direct people to your social media pages. Oh, and that's the other thing, the more in-your-face and engaged you are on Facebook, Twitter, Instagram, and whatever other crazy new social media entities exist by the time you're running for office, the better.

Never forget, though: you're almost certainly losing this campaign if you don't show up in person, shake hands, kiss babies, and tell people why you deserve this office. Have conversations! Ask people what they want, and then refine your messaging.

STEP 9: GET. OUT. THE. VOTE.

Just because someone was like, "Yeah, for sure, you got it, coroner . . . whatever that is," before they shut their door in your face does *not* mean they're showing up on Election Day. Even if they do, there's no guarantee they'll remember your name! Make a concerted effort in the weeks and finally days before the election to knock on those same doors again with a friendly, "hey, remember me, Election Day's coming up, here is my name, don't forget! Love you, bye." Print mailers that remind voters when Election Day is, that tell them who to call to figure out their polling place, and that have a big ol' picture of grinning you with your name in bold. If you can afford a campaign commercial, the weeks before an election are a good time to creep into homes across your county by way of the television screen. And remember those die-hard supporters, volunteers, and staffers you've acquired over the past few months? Now's the time for them to stand on street corners holding signs with your name on them and hoping that passing cars give a little honk of support.

STEP 10: VOTE FOR YOURSELF. THEN WAIT AND SEE.

Admit it, this is going to be so cool. You're going to walk into your polling place, request a ballot, see your name on there next to that office that you've worked so hard for,

and *vote for yourself.* I mean, okay, you don't *have* to vote for yourself. After this point, depending on your state or local laws, you can probably join your supporters near the entrance of various polling places with those big ol' signs with your name on them to remind people, one last time, who they want as coroner, sheriff, mayor, whathaveyou. Then go wait for the results to come in.

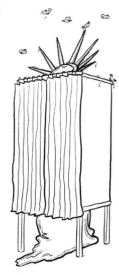

GO FORTH AND PROSPER

Why did we write this book?

The United States of America is a nation that refused to meaningfully *start* without the establishment of civil liberties. The conversation about how we ought to be as a nation was predicated on the preservation of sovereignty for the states and freedom for the masses. If that is the country in which we live, if the government was built for you, then why do you need to know any of this stuff?

Well. Because the United States is not the paper on which our doctrines were written. The rights reserved for the citizens of this country are a wonderful concept, but it doesn't matter how many of those rights have been codified or added to our revered Constitution if they are not then upheld by the fallible, corruptible, forgetful, sometimes malicious people who run this place. The system and its rules and regulations can be a beautiful thing if stewarded well and wielded properly. There's only one way to know if that's happening or not, though. You have to know what your rights are and how those stewards of democracy are supposed to behave. Then you have to call it out when you witness or experience injustice or maladministration.

That's why we wrote this book. So that you'd have the tools to enjoy your liberties, exercise your responsibilities, and help to ensure that this democratic experiment is what it purports to be. A Republic, if we can keep it.

APPENDIX

POP QUIZ!

You didn't think we'd let you duck out of here without a final homework assignment, did you? Now, are the answers to the following questions contained in these very pages? They are. And nobody will know if you sneak a peek back. Nobody, dear reader, but you. And you have to live with you *all the time*. So be your own valiant creature of integrity and spring this pop quiz on yourself to see what you've learned.

1. Up until 1917, the Senate permitted a filibuster to go on *ad infinitum*, which really threw a wrench in the gears of Congress. They finally got their act together and created a process by which filibuster could be ended with a two-thirds, and later three-fifths, vote. What is the name of the **motion** that ends that windbaggery? _____

2. On a similar subject, **what is it called** when the Senate votes to change their rules out of the blue, a tactic which was first used in 2013 to forbid the filibuster when it came to executive and federal judicial appointments (the Supreme Court being the one exception to the new rule)? _____

_____

3. Spelling doesn't count. **What is the name of the writ** that one petitions for to get a case heard by the Supreme Court?

And for a bonus point, how many of the nine Justices are required to grant this writ?

4. What's the first word of, respectively, the Declaration of Independence, the Constitution, and the First Amendment in the Bill of Rights? _____, _____, _____

5. One of the most influential roles in the Executive Branch requires that you are a proper civilian, in this case meaning you cannot have served in the military for at least seven years, before you take the gig. The primary office building for this department is the largest in the world. **Name this department secretary.** _____

6. Fill in the blank! Your state gets as many electoral votes as it has _____

7. The Constitution has seven articles and twenty-seven amendments. **Which one of these** explicitly grants citizens the right to vote? _____

8. The first hundred days of any presidency are scrutinized by the public and press alike. We think of whatever happens in the first three some-odd months as being an indication of what's to come, a place where mettle is proved. But *why*? **Name the president who gave us this first hundred days notion** by getting a whopping fifteen sweeping bills through Congress by June in his first term. _____

_____

9. We touched on many SCOTUS cases in the book, but **which case** was the granddaddy of them all, giving the Court the power to interpret the Constitution? _____

_____

10. Theodore Roosevelt was instrumental in changing the look of federalism in this fair country of ours. He coined **a term to describe the leveraging of popularity and power** to influence Congress and expand federal power. What is this now well-used expression? _____

___

11. The United States Constitution is our fair nation's *second* constitution. The first one was written over the course of 1776 and 1777, lasted just over a decade, and was called *what*? _____

_____

12. **What is the name of the Act**, passed in 1973 and routinely ignored by sitting presidents, that requires the commander in chief to notify Congress when deploying troops? _____

_____

13. **Name the *two* types of nominating elections** that states use to determine who will end up on the ballot. _____

_____ and _____

_____

14. The world "slavery" appears in the Constitution only once, and it's in the amendment that served to abolish the institution. **Which of the Reconstruction Amendments** abolished slavery and involuntary servitude? _____

_____

15. Fill in the blank! What are the magic words that you can use in most states to cast your vote on election day even if you don't have proof of voter eligibility? "I request a _____ _____ and receipt as is required by law."

ANSWER KEY ON PAGE 351

HAIL TO THE CHIEF: PRESIDENTIAL FUN FACTS

Volumes have been written about each of these presidents, but here are some facts you might just not know.

George Washington (1789–1797)

The historians at Mount Vernon do all they can to disabuse us of the many Washington myths: he never came clean about chopping down a cherry tree, he never threw a silver dollar across the Potomac, he didn't wear a wig, let alone a wig for his wig. And he didn't have wooden teeth. They were false teeth though—he'd lost most of his real teeth by the time he was thirty. After his inauguration the final tooth came out, a premolar, and he gifted it to his lifelong dentist. His false teeth were likely made from human teeth, hippo ivory, and metal. As they were difficult to keep clean, some suppose the rumor of wooden teeth came from their appearance.

John Adams (1797–1801)

Our first vice president and our second commander in chief, John Adams was utterly devoted to the cause of American independence. And hard cider. The guy raved about cider. He professed to drinking a gill of it each morning before breakfast (that's a quarter pint) and lauded its healthful properties. In letters to fellow Harvard graduate Dr. Benjamin Waterhouse, he wrote, "I have always believed that the almost universal health among the Students, was to be ascribed, next to early rising and beef and mutton Pies at Commons, to the free Use of Cider and the very moderate Use of Wine and ardent Spirits."

Thomas Jefferson (1801–1809)

T. Jeff was *obsessed* with mammoths. Just mad about the things. He wrote letters about them, he collected their teeth, he even advocated in the 1780s that they *still lived and roamed the Great Plains in secret.* Sure, the expedition of Lewis and Clark was all about taking land, but it was also a hunt for mammoth bones. Really.

James Madison (1809–1817)

Madison was our shortest president at five foot four, a full two inches shorter than Benjamin Harrison. But it's unfair to speak of the "father of the Constitution" and just mention his height. We should also mention that in 1777 he lost an election to the Virginia House of Delegates, a loss he would later blame entirely on the fact that he didn't give free booze to the public on Election Day, a practice known at the time as "swilling the planters with bumbo." The other guy? Who won? Yeah, he swilled those planters with bumbo, and he swilled them good. But Madison wasn't deterred from political life, and in 1780 he became the youngest member of the Continental Congress.

James Monroe (1817–1825)

In 1820, Monroe was running for reelection. And in a turn of events not seen before or since, he was the *only presidential candidate on the ballot.* At the time, the Federalist Party had been steadily declining, and Monroe was part of the flashy new Democratic-Republicans. And by 1820, the Federalists were doing so poorly that they didn't even have enough support to get a candidate on the ballot. And yes, he won, but he didn't get every single electoral vote. One elector, William Plumer from New Hampshire, cast his vote for Monroe's secretary of state, a young fellow by the name of John Quincy Adams.

John Quincy Adams (1825–1829)

We've been in the habit of legacy presidential candidates for a while in the U.S. John Quincy was the oldest son of Abigail and John Adams (our second president). This creature of familial habit made a point of meticulously documenting his life in daily diaries, from age twelve until he died. Which is how we know the man loved a good early morning skinny dip.

As long as the weather allowed for it, J.Q. would wake up super early—4 or 5 a.m.—walk two miles, and find himself on the banks of the Potomac River. That's where he would strip down to his birthday suit, splash around for a bit, and walk home.

Sometimes he got his Dutch diplomat pal to go with him. Apparently his friends and doctors tended to think it was all a bit much, but he kept at it, writing, "the art of swimming ought in my opinion to be taught as a regular branch of education." He did not specify whether those lessons were to be conducted in the buff.

Andrew Jackson (1829–1837)

At Jackson's funeral, his pet parrot Poll (initially his wife Rachel's) got excited and, according to Reverend William Menefee Norment, "let loose perfect gusts of cuss words . . . swearing so loud and long as to disturb the people and had to be carried from the house."

Martin Van Buren (1837–1841)

Our eighth president, nicknamed "the little magician," has a wonderful pair of firsts: He was the first president to be born in the United States of America, and also our first (and so far only) president who spoke English as a second language. He grew up in Kinderhook, New York, in a Dutch-speaking household.

William Henry Harrison (1841)

There's not much to say about the Harrison administration, because he contracted pneumonia shortly after his inauguration and died. His term was thirty-one days, the number of words in this paragraph.

John Tyler (1841–1845)

Tyler was the first to ascend to the office of the presidency by means other than an election. When William Henry Harrison died, there was a constitutional question: Did Article II imply that Tyler become the president in name? Or did the powers of the president just extend to the VP? The former was where we landed, Tyler so insistent on it that any letters addressed to "Vice President Tyler" were returned unopened.

James K. Polk (1845–1849)

Polk is called the first "dark horse" president, someone relatively unknown who wins a race. It took nine votes at the Democratic nominating convention for him to secure the party's nomination, and he won against the Whig Henry Clay by a very narrow margin. When Polk was told that he'd secured the nomination, he *said* he hadn't even wanted to be president (we'll never know the truth of this) and vowed to serve only one term, which he did. He had four goals for his administration: lower tariffs, acquire a bunch of Oregon, acquire California from Mexico, and reestablish the Independent Treasury System. All of which he did.

Zachary Taylor (1849–1850)

Taylor was nicknamed "Old Rough and Ready," and boy did he look it. He'd been a career officer in the Army and he just had the appearance of having seen some *stuff,* you know? Mussed hair, wrinkled uniform. Though he identified strongly as an Independent, Taylor did finally concede to identifying as a Whig in order to receive the party's nomination in 1848. The actual receipt of the nomination was a bit of an issue, though.

Taylor did not attend the June 1848 convention, so the party mailed him notification of his nomination. At the time, the postal system operated in such a way that the person on the receiving end was the one to pay the postage (a nineteenth-century-day "I'll accept the charges," which, yes, we know means nothing to anyone born after the advent of the cell phone). Taylor, being a military hero after his show in the Mexican-American War, got a lot of fan mail. Rather than pay the postage, he returned most of his great deal of mail to sender. This included the Whig nomination. Taylor did not discover he was the presidential nominee until July.

An ignoble end; Taylor died about a year into his first term from digestive issues after consuming a staggering quantity of raw milk and iced fruit.

Millard Fillmore (1850–1853)

Okay, *first of all,* Millard Fillmore straight up looks like a Baldwin Brother. Like for real. And though he regularly appears at the bottom of lists ranking our presidents, Fillmore once spent Christmas morning closest to the flames at the end of a bucket brigade attempting to put out a fire at the Library of Congress. Thirty-five thousand books were lost in the fire, and Fillmore pushed Congress to appropriate funds to replace them all. While he was at it, he got the cash to establish the first permanent White House library. Oh also, he married his *teacher.* I *mean.* Book-loving, teacher-seducing Baldwin dead-ringer? You know what? Milquetoast or not, Fillmore's all right.

Franklin Pierce (1853–1857)

Pierce had quite possibly the saddest inauguration in U.S. history. He and his wife, Jane, had already suffered the loss of two of their three boys due to illness, but within weeks of being elected, Pierce's surviving son, Benny, died in a train accident. Some Pierce trivia that's unrelated to tragedy or alcoholism: He's the only president to use the word "affirm" instead of "swear" upon taking the Oath of Office, which he did on a book of law. Also, he was the first president to have a Christmas tree in the White House!

James Buchanan (1857–1861)

Buchanan was a slippery one. He defended the constitutionality of slavery and supported secession, then supported Lincoln during the Civil War. It seems like he probably thought that, if mostly avoided, slavery would just go away. For being a northerner who accepted southern policies, he was nicknamed "Doughface." So, not great. But tell ya what, Buchanan could drink you under the table. He reportedly kept a well-stocked wine cellar and would drink two or three bottles, along with some whiskey, in a single sitting without losing his composure. Those who tried to keep up failed miserably.

Abraham Lincoln (1861–1865)

He's routinely rated as the greatest, most impressive, most effective president this nation has ever seen. Yet nowhere in that list is "knock-down, drag-out wrestling champ." What gives?

Lincoln's stellar wrestling career first made the papers after his campaign opponent, Stephen Douglas, brought it up during one of their famed debates. "Lincoln is one of those peculiar men who perform with admirable skill everything which they undertake," Douglas said. "He could beat any of the boys wrestling, or running a foot race, in pitching quoits or tossing a copper, could ruin more liquor than all the boys of the town together."

Lincoln reportedly lost in only one of three hundred recorded wrestling matches, and was famed in his small town of New Salem, Illinois, for supposedly taking on the town bully and knocking the guy out cold. So yeah, Lincoln was basically the

Daniel LaRusso of his generation. In 1992, he was officially inducted into the Wrestling Hall of Fame.

Andrew Johnson (1865–1869)

Johnson, successor to Abraham Lincoln upon the president's assassination, dodged a literal bullet in order to become our seventeenth. The night John Wilkes Booth murdered Lincoln, a man named George Atzerodt was tasked with knocking on Johnson's hotel room door and shooting him point blank. But Atzerodt couldn't work up the courage. When he finally confessed to his role in the plot, he was sentenced to death by hanging. Andrew Johnson signed the order.

Ulysses S. Grant (1869–1877)

Grant's real name was Hiram Ulysses Grant. The "S" was a mistake made by the Congressman who nominated him to attend West Point and it just *stuck*. Grant eventually gave into it, but we like to think of it as a stylistic choice, like when Michael Andrew Fox changed his middle initial to "*J*" so that headlines wouldn't read "Michael's a Fox!" Grant, by the way, was a war hero whose memoirs detailing his experiences in the Civil War made him a best seller (though only after his death). His publisher? Mark Twain.

Rutherford B. Hayes (1877–1881)

Hayes has gone down in history as a little-remembered president, but he ascended to the White House in one of the most contested, hostile elections in America. After the votes were tallied the predicted winner, Samuel Tilden, was one electoral vote short. With parties in four states claiming that their candidate had won (an impossibility), Congress and the Supreme

Court intervened and awarded the contested votes to Hayes, on the condition that federal troops were removed from the South, where they had been enforcing civil liberties of newly enfranchised Black voters. The fallout of this "corrupt bargain" (as it became known) was so severe that Hayes had to be sworn in via a secret ceremony in the White House Red Room.

James Abram Garfield (1881)

Garfield is possibly best known for having been shot four months into his presidency and dying of infection two and a half months later. His very election was nearly thrown into peril, however, when mere weeks before the election a letter surfaced in which he voiced his support for Chinese laborers in the United States. At a time when much of the country feared what immigrants would do to employment, this could've dealt a real blow to his campaign. If he'd actually written it, that is. Turns out the whole thing was fraudulent, planted by Democrats in order to discredit Garfield. The candidate waited a while before denying he'd written it because, frankly, he just couldn't remember.

Chester A. Arthur (1881–1885)

Elegant Arthur was quite the fop about town when he ascended to the presidency. He got the job after Andrew Garfield was assassinated and became the second VP in history to come by the gig incidentally.

At the time, the White House was in such bad shape that people actually blamed it for Garfield's inability to recuperate.

When Arthur—a regular Gatsby, who loved fine accoutrements and lavish parties—moved in, he made renovations a priority. Step One: Clean house. Sell off a bunch of stuff, including a pair of Lincoln's pants. Step Two: Hire Louis Comfort Tiffany (yes, that Tiffany) to go to town on the mansion and put a bunch of really beautiful glass everywhere. Step Three: Invite a bunch of fancies over and earn yourself the nickname "The Gentleman Boss."

Grover Cleveland (1885–1889, 1893–1897)

Cleveland is the only president in history to serve two non-consecutive terms. As in he tried for reelection while incumbent and lost, and then ran again later and won. Cleveland is considered a man of remarkable honesty, integrity, and common sense. Which is perhaps why, after he played executioner for the first time, he was "a sick man for several days thereafter." That's right. Cleveland is the only president to have ever hanged a man. In fact, he hanged two, as Sheriff of Erie County in New York.

Benjamin Harrison (1889–1893)

The grandson of William Henry Harrison, Benjamin Harrison was a president of unprecedented economic legislation that included the Sherman Anti-Trust Act, which regulated competition and prohibited trusts. But the best thing about Benjamin Harrison? He was the first president to live in a White House lit by electric lamps, only he and his wife were so afraid of light switches that they tended to just go to sleep with the lights on.

William McKinley (1897–1901)

The third American president to be assassinated, McKinley was shot by anarchist Leon Czolgosz at the Temple of Music in the Pan American Exposition in Buffalo. McKinley's secretary was so worried something bad would go down at the Temple of Music that he took it off his agenda *two times*. But McKinley was not to be deterred. As he lay bleeding, the crowd descended upon Czolgosz, and McKinley apparently cried, "Don't let them hurt him . . . it must have been some poor, misguided fellow."

Though there was a Secret Service at the time, it mostly dealt with investigating counterfeiting. The procedure for protecting the president tended to be your basic "hands where I can see 'em." But the day of McKinley's assassination was so hot that the empty hand rule was waived to allow for handkerchiefs—the perfect place to hide a gun. After McKinley's death, the Secret Service was formally tasked with being the president's protector. They had their work cut out for them on the first go-around: it was their job to keep Teddy Roosevelt alive.

Theodore Roosevelt (1901–1909)

Teddy Roosevelt was a *tough cookie*. Having suffered a sickly childhood, he resolved to maintain health through rigorous physical activity and boy, did he ever. After his first wife and mother died on the same day (Roosevelt's diary entry read simply, "The light has gone out of my life"), he took to the prairies for a solo sojourn. Stopping at a hotel for the night, Roosevelt was confronted by a "shabby individual in a broad hat with a cocked gun in each hand," who made the mistake of calling Teddy "four-eyes." Oops.

With the cowboy's guns pointed right at him, Teddy hits him with a right hook, then a left, then a right! The guns fire as the bully goes down, smacking his head on the bar as he does. Teddy then drags him out to the shed for the night. By the next morning, the guy had left town. *Don't mess with Teddy.*

William Howard Taft (1909–1913)

If you've heard the tale of Taft getting stuck in the White House bathtub, please know historians agree that charming footnote is probably a complete fabrication. But it's okay! The president who only ever wanted to be a Supreme Court Justice has some lovely, true footnotes, including one of the worst PR disasters in history. Seeing the popularity of Roosevelt's eponymous Teddy Bear, Taft's campaign managers tried to replicate his success by creating a plush toy based on Taft's favorite meal: a roast possum served on a platter of taters. Needless to say, the "Billy Possum" toy was an absolute flop.

Woodrow Thomas Wilson (1913–1921)

For a president who witnessed the Civil War, Wilson threw a lot of wrenches in the fight for civil rights in the United States. His parents *were* Confederate supporters. He allowed segregation at the governmental level and once dismissed a Black civil rights leader, William Trotter, from a meeting at the White House simply because Trotter disagreed with Wilson's views on segregation. The twenty-eighth president *did* support the Nineteenth Amendment and a woman's right to vote and establish the League of Nations, but he also screened *Song of the South* in the newly established White House screening room.

Warren Gamaliel Harding (1921–1923)

Harding had something of a temper (and a wandering eye; he had two confirmed affairs while serving as president and there are letters to prove it). He reportedly once threw a colonel against the wall after learning of corruption in the Veteran's Bureau, calling him a "yellow rat." And once, after reading in the *Washington Post* a bad review of a recital his daughter gave, Harding wrote to the reviewer saying that he'd like to meet him, and that when he did, the man would "need a new nose, a lot of beefsteak for black eyes, and perhaps a supporter below!"

Calvin John Coolidge (1923–1929)

Coolidge was a cold, puritanical New Englander with the kind of wit that you might miss the first time around. He was nicknamed "Silent Cal," and once said to a woman who vowed to get more than two words out of him at a dinner party, "You lose." After getting his first paycheck from the Treasury Department, he simply said to the messenger, "Call again." As vice president, presiding over the Senate, Coolidge was asked to deal with one senator who was telling another to go to hell. The story goes that Coolidge determined that the offending senator had the right to lob the provocation, but informed the offended that he did not "*have* to go." A bone-dry Yankee heart if we've ever seen one.

Herbert Clark Hoover (1929–1933)

Hoover's campaign slogan was "a chicken in every pot and a car in every garage." Though he doesn't tend to make the top of the presidential rankings, Hoover was considered a great humanitarian. Appointed by Woodrow Wilson to head the U.S. Food Administration, the self-made millionaire led an effort to get about a hundred thousand Americans out of Europe at the start of World War I, established a relief commission in order to feed millions of Belgians, and even met with the German army to ensure food delivery. The agency was renamed the American Relief Administration and prevented the starvation of hundreds of millions of people in post-war Europe. All of this without ever having been elected to office. In fact, when he won the presidency, it was Hoover's first-ever elected position.

Franklin Delano Roosevelt (1933–1945)

The longest-serving president, the one who triggered a constitutional amendment that would ensure that no one ever reigned that long again, the one who won by a landslide every time, was wheelchair-bound most of his life. FDR suffered a bout of polio as a child that left him paralyzed from the waist down. He could walk short distances with the help of braces and a cane, but tended to rely on the wheelchair. Thing is, the American public never realized the extent of his handicap. The media pretty much kept it a secret in a move of deference that is practically unimaginable today. You'll notice that in the bulk of pictures of FDR, he's either at a podium or in a car.

Harry S. Truman (1945–1953)

Truman became president after the sudden death of Franklin Delano Roosevelt and would go on to authorize one of the most controversial actions ever taken in wartime—the dropping of atomic bombs on Hiroshima and Nagasaki. But, despite being vice president, Truman did not learn of the *existence* of the atomic bomb until after he was sworn into office. Just moments after he took the oath, the secretary of war at the time pulled the new president aside and informed him of a little something called the Manhattan Project. Four months later, the United States dropped two of the "most terrible weapon[s] ever known in human history," causing total devastation and bringing an end to World War II.

Dwight Eisenhower (1953–1961)

Ike is such a weird nickname, right? How do you get "Ike" from "Dwight"? Well, you don't. Turns out "Ike" comes from Eisenhower (still, though, how?), and the whole family went by Ike! Anyway, voters liked Ike, and Ike liked smoking. A lot. Three to four packs a day a lot. His first attempt at quitting was a total disaster. So instead, he played this sick little game where he kept cigarettes *everywhere* and offered them to *everyone*. He'd light someone up and think to himself, well, at least you're not doing what *that* guy is doing. And that worked. The mind is a strange thing. Especially the mind of a president.

John Fitzgerald Kennedy (1961–1963)

JFK suffered from severe health problems most of his life—problems so severe that he was given Last Rites (the final ministrations given to a Catholic before they die) *four times.* These issues ranged from Addison's disease, an adrenal condition, to one of his legs being shorter than the other. You'd probably never have known it to look at him, though, in part because he glided through the pain on a cocktail of amphetamines and painkillers administered by a Dr. Max Jacobson—more commonly known in Hollywood circles as "Dr. Feelgood."

Lyndon Baines Johnson (1963–1969)

Though LBJ didn't win the presidency (he succeeded John F. Kennedy after the president was assassinated), he was one of the more legislatively effective in history. This is in part due to a tactic referred to only as the "Treatment." This included flattery and vague threats, but perhaps the most effective of the strategies was Johnson's habit of invading personal space in order to get what he wanted. He was six foot four and used that considerable height to his advantage. When advocating for what he wanted, Johnson would occasionally get inches from his target, towering over them while he told them exactly what they'd be doing for him. There are pictures of this. Frankly, it looks terrifying.

Richard Nixon (1969–1974)

Sure, Clinton played the sax, Chester A. Arthur (supposedly) played the banjo, and Warren G. Harding played just about everything, but Nixon was one of our more musical presidents. A year after losing the 1960 election to Kennedy, he played his own composition, a piano concerto, on *The Tonight Show* with Jack Paar. Neither Nixon nor his many advisors thought it would be a good idea, but it showed a relaxed, even charming side of the would-be president. Media theorist Marshall McLuhan wrote of the performance, "a few timely touches like this would have quite altered the result of the Kennedy-Nixon campaign."

Gerald Rudolph Ford (1974–1977)

Gerald Ford was never actually elected into the office of VP *or* POTUS. He was appointed by Nixon when his VP, Spiro Agnew, resigned after being indicted for bribery. Ford then stepped into the role after the president's resignation in 1974. But you know what he *was* elected? Most Valuable Player. Ford was so skilled a football player at the University of Michigan that he was offered a place on both the Detroit Lions *and* the Green Bay Packers. He opted to go to Yale Law instead. That jock history came back to bite him once he made it to Congress, though, when Lyndon B. Johnson said of him that he'd "played too much football without a helmet."

Jimmy Carter (1977–1981)

Much of Jimmy Carter's best work was done after he left the White House. He won the Nobel Peace Prize, founded a center to battle disease and advocate for peace, and built homes for Habitat for Humanity. But one unique accomplishment was well before he took office: He was the first U.S. president to be born in a hospital.

Ronald Reagan (1981–1989)

The Teflon President would have fit in pretty well in modern-day Bushwick—dude was all about astrology. His chief of staff spilled the jellybeans in his tell-all *For the Record,* saying that "virtually every major move" that Reagan made during the CoS's time in the White House was first cleared with an astrologer in San Francisco: Ms. Joan Quigley.

Quigley claimed to have used horoscopes to help the White House time speeches, press conferences, Air Force One trips—she even recommended that Reagan's second swearing-in ceremony be timed for 11:56:50 to make the best of planetary alignments.

George H. W. Bush (1989–1993)

Human, all too human Papa Bush overexerted himself on a trip to Asia in 1992 and wound up vomiting in the lap of the prime minister of Japan.

After a twelve-day, not-super-successful trip, Bush was somewhere between the second and third courses when he turned white as a sheet, fainted, fell over, and lost his raw salmon with caviar directly onto Prime Minister Kiichi Miyazawa. He was the first president to do so!

Bush returned home to low approval ratings and the mocking of American comedians everywhere. Meanwhile, in Japan, the incident provided late-night fodder for years, and even resulted in a new slang term, Bushu-suru, "do the Bush thing."

William Jefferson Clinton (1993–2001)

The Man from Hope ran an infamously scandalous White House always while managing to distract, deflect, and charm his way out of everything from a reporter's line of questioning to an impeachment hearing. Before he even landed in the White House, his campaign struggling under the revelation that he'd had an affair with Arkansas cabaret singer Gennifer Flowers, Clinton went for something wildly distracting. He got a spot on the late-night *Arsenio Hall Show,* borrowed a pair of Ray-Bans, picked up a saxophone, and played along to Elvis Presley's "Heartbreak Hotel." The crowd, and the voters, loved it. Clinton climbed in the polls and made it into the presidency.

George Walker Bush (2001–2009)

When George Bush left office in 2009, he said of his time there that the presidency was a "joyful experience," but that "nothing compares with a Texas sunset." And then he leaned *hard* into aesthetic pleasure. Our forty-third president has become a prolific oil painter, and he's actually pretty good. He started out with dogs and world leaders, dabbled a bit with bathroom self-portraits (*yeah*) and then moved on to paintings of physically or emotionally wounded veterans. Bush says that getting into oil painting changed his life. Like, as much as being Leader of the Free World, or . . . ?

Barack Obama (2009–2017)

He's regularly referred to as the coolest president, and I'm not about to take that away from him. His Secret Service codename was "Renegade." He's really good at basketball. He freely admits to smoking weed, and not just that, but shouting "intercepted!" and taking an extra hit when a joint made the rounds. He can bench press two hundred pounds! But the coolest thing about Obama? He can admit he married up. "Michelle's like Beyoncé in that song, 'Let me upgrade ya!' She upgraded me. There's no doubt I'm a better man having spent time with Michelle."

Donald Trump (2017–?)

There are a whole lotta firsts in the Trump administration, but here's the one we're going with: He is the first president since Polk to not have a pet.

POP QUIZ ANSWERS

1. Cloture
2. Nuclear Option
3. Certiorari, four
4. When, We, Congress
5. Secretary of Defense
6. Members of Congress (Senators and Representatives)
7. None, trick question, it's not in there
8. Franklin Delano Roosevelt
9. *Marbury v. Madison*
10. The Bully Pulpit
11. The Articles of Confederation
12. The War Powers Act
13. Primaries and caucuses
14. The Thirteenth Amendment
15. Provisional ballot

ACKNOWLEDGMENTS

We are indebted to the minds who lent us their understanding of this nation. Here's to you, Linda Monk, Alvin Tillery, Danielle Allen, Woody Holton, and Keneshia Grant.

Thanks to Dan Cassino for making sure we got it right and your infinite patience in explaining this country to us. Over and over and over again.

Erika Janik, were it not for your daily guidance, casual brilliance, and willingness to put up with us, this book never would've happened.

Maureen McMurray, you're the whole reason we fell down the civics rabbit hole. Thanks for the push.

Logan Shannon, thank you for writing "Schoolhouse Rock for adults" on a Post-it, changing all our lives.

Thanks to our lovely agent, Julia Eagleton, who found us. And to everyone at Celadon for their time, energy, and effort in helping us create this book.

Hannah wants to thank Sylvia Wozny, who always calls bull

and made this book a little better every time she did it. And to those dazzling people who are kind enough to be in my karass and share their wit—I hold you dear, Martha Clark, Jack McCarthy, Olympia Shannon, Anna Rogovoy, Bobby Delanghe, Colin Hinckley, Andrew Duff, and Josh Max.

Nick wants to thank his sister, Cami Capodice, who bore the brunt of a hundred calls asking about substantive vs. procedural due process, and his mother, Cynthia Brophy, for never letting the truth get in the way of a joke. Finally, he owes everything to the most generous and creative minds he has had the opportunity to know and love: Brenna Farrell, John-Henry Boudreaux, Frank Boudreaux, Kate Kita, Megan Gaffney, Frank Philbrick, Annie Polland, Jason Eisner, Tom Bouman, and Joe Randazzo. And, always, the Flanks and the Shanks.

Tom wants to thank his family—those who get Hungarian jokes, and those who only pretend to, which is really the same thing. Andras, Jane, Katalin, you made me who I am, and everything I make is yours. Can there be anyone in the world who's kinder, smarter, or lovelier than Marissa Wolf? (That's a rhetorical question.) Can I express the adoration I feel for Elijah Wolf Toro in Lego? (That's a real one.)

ABOUT THE AUTHORS

Hannah McCarthy has written about the opioid crisis, professional wrestling, urban cavers, and the arts for various publications, but this is her first book. She lives in Concord, New Hampshire, though her heart's in Brooklyn.

Nick Capodice wrote short fiction with The Engine, an artistic development utility in Brooklyn. He developed and led tours on NYC history, beer, and food. Nick plays harmonica with The Flanks, and he always will.

Tom Toro is a cartoonist for *The New Yorker* and other publications. He is the author and illustrator of the children's picture book *How to Potty Train Your Porcupine* and the cartoon collection *Tiny Hands*. He lives in Portland, Oregon—a city that would have been named Boston if a coin flip had gone differently.

CELADON
BOOKS
———
NEW YORK

Founded in 2017, Celadon Books, a division of
Macmillan Publishers, publishes a highly curated list
of twenty to twenty-five new titles a year. The list of
both fiction and nonfiction is eclectic and focuses
on publishing commercial and literary books and
discovering and nurturing talent.